Your One-Stop Guide to
Heaven, Hell and Purgatory

Your One-Stop Guide to Heaven, Hell and Purgatory

BILL DODDS

CHARIS

SERVANT PUBLICATIONS
ANN ARBOR, MICHIGAN

Charis Books is an imprint of Servant Publications especially designed to serve
Roman Catholics.

The Scripture quotations contained herein are from the New Revised Standard
Version of the Bible: Catholic edition copyright 1993 and 1989 by the Division
of Christian Education of the National Council of the Churches of Christ in the
USA. Used by permission. All rights reserved.

Servant Publications
P.O. Box 8617
Ann Arbor, MI 48107

Cover design by Hile Illustration and Design-Ann Arbor, Michigan

01 02 03 04 10 9 8 7 6 5 4 3 2 1

Printed in the United States of America
ISBN 1-56955-228-2

LIBRARY OF CONGRESS CATALOGING-IN-PUBLICATION DATA

Dodds, Bill.
    Your one-stop guide to heaven, hell, and purgatory / Bill Dodds.
        p. cm.
    Includes index.
    ISBN 1-56955-228-2 (alk. paper)
    1. Future life—Catholic Church. 2. Catholic Church—Doctrines. I. Title.
    BT902 .D63 2001
    236'.2—dc21

                                                                    2001017363

Dedication

To the Sulpician Fathers
who were my teachers
(any mistakes in this book are mine, not theirs)

Contents

Chapter One

As Certain as Death and ... Latin

You're going to die.

You. Reading these words.

You are going to cease living. It's a done deal. Las Vegas wouldn't take money on your body living forever, no matter what odds you offered.

I'm going to die, too. There's no way around this. If there were, someone a lot smarter than either of us would have figured it out a long time ago. So trust me, it's going to happen. On some particular day of the week, some date of the month, some year, you will stop living.

And then ... what? The world will continue to spin. The sun will rise and set. The tides will go in and out. The seasons will change. Birds will continue to sing, rush-hour traffic will continue to snarl, and your loved ones, though grieving, will begin to move on. Life will continue. You just won't be around to experience it.

We're All Gonna Die

I'm not sure when that thought really occurred to me. Certainly as someone who was baptized Catholic as an infant and raised in a strong Catholic family, the concept of death wasn't foreign to me. Like all little Catholic kids learning the Hail Mary at their mother's knee, I said, "pray for us sinners, now and at the hour of our death. Amen."

By teaching me that prayer, my mother and my Church were preparing me for the fact that the hour was coming when I would die. Back then, those were just words.

Yes, Grandma had died, and that was very sad. Old people died.

Yes, cousin Eddie had died in the war and that was a tragedy. Soldiers died in wars.

Yes, there are people who die in car accidents and when lightning strikes and from chronic illness and all the rest. But ... well, as a kid I figured I was immune from it all. Right?

"How Long, Pray Cataline ..."

I don't remember when I began associating death with Latin class. "Third-high" (junior year) Latin was just something that happened. But, like death, it happened to someone else.

Or so I thought.

I entered the seminary in ninth grade and stayed through my sophomore year of college, from 1966 to 1972. It was an interesting time; in many ways, it was in one era and out the other.

The Second Vatican Council—with all its sweeping changes—had convened from 1962 to 1965. Many of the new or renewed ideas and practices were implemented during my seminary years. One practice that did *not* change was Latin instruction. Four years of Latin in high school. The junior-year teacher, the one who taught "third-high Latin," was a legend.

As with any all-boys school, my seminary had its share of hazing. There was a definite pecking order among the students. Some sophomores delighted in making life miserable for certain freshmen. Just as the juniors had made *their* lives miserable the previous year. And so on.

Theoretically, this meant that the juniors were even tougher than the sophomores, who were incredibly tough on the freshmen. Which made it all the more startling when juniors would come into the refectory during lunch and tell amazing tales of what had happened that morning in third-high Latin.

We sat in assigned seats for meals. Two members of each class made up a table of eight. We freshmen were at the far end, but we could listen in on what the big kids were saying. We could see the concern on their faces and hear the strain in their voices.

We knew these were no wimps. These were tough kids. These were smart kids. And, yes, some of these were holy kids. However, they all had the same message: Third-high Latin was grinding them down. The professor was *that* tough. And the ultimate horror of it all was getting "the call." We soon learned that this referred to some poor individual being singled out to translate Cicero's orations for the majority of the fifty-minute period.

We had all had demanding teachers. But ... but these upper classmen were clearly shaken by what they were going through, clearly working incredibly hard to prepare for their eventual grilling. Clearly hoping, and probably even praying, it didn't soon happen to them.

The seniors would nod, "I told you so" on their faces if not on their lips. Fourth-high Latin students were in their second year with this priest, and they had their own stories—as well as legends—to tell.

All this was interesting to witness as a freshman, and even more enjoyable, as a sophomore, to see some former bullies getting a little payback. But as my sophomore year ended it occurred to me, in a flash of fear, that come the fall, my own class would be taking third-high Latin.

I would be in that room.

Nonsense, I had always concluded. That's not going to happen. There would be a different professor. There would be a change in the curriculum. There would be ... something so it never happened to me. It did, of course. Although, by some miracle, in two years I never got the full "call," I had my share of terror.

It wasn't until years later that another lesson dawned on me, a basic truth that had nothing to do with Cicero or Virgil. One, I'm sure, that the teacher had never intended: Death is like third-high Latin.

In my youth, it seemed distant. As I got older, I assumed somehow I would escape it. Now I know that's not the case. My time, my turn, will come.

And so will yours.

What Is Death?

Death is the great equalizer, striking down prince and pauper alike. Sometimes unexpectedly and seemingly without regard to rank or hardship, virtue or vice.

Death is also the great mystery. All human beings step up to that door, and through that door—alone—and then what? Never mind what's on the other side, what does even passing through that doorway mean? What *is* death?

God created each of us with two parts, two components—the body and the soul. The body is the part of you that can be seen and touched. It's the part that eats food and grows bigger and skins its knees, the part that gets sick and gets hurt in accidents and which, ultimately, stops functioning. When we die, the soul—the part of us that lives forever—leaves the body. (We'll talk more about the soul in the next chapter.)

We human beings are the only creatures who realize that at some point our bodies are going to quit. This is one of the abilities and gifts that distinguishes us from all the animals on earth. A dog doesn't know its days are numbered, even if that number is in dog years. A squirrel doesn't comprehend that it has only a few summers to gather those nuts, a few winters to eat them. A butterfly, a blade of grass, a microscopic bacterium can't foresee that it will be here today and gone tomorrow.

We alone have the ability to worry about our mortality.

We alone ask why we have to die.

And we alone question what happens next. We're the only ones who can put a thought into words: Where has my loved one gone? Where, someday, will I go?

The Big Questions

Since these questions are a universal concern, every world religion, one way or another, attempts to address them.

Some say after life on earth there is nothing. You simply, and sadly, wink out of existence.

Others teach that you begin another life here on earth, in a different form.

Where, exactly, will you be? Your next stop could be:

—Heaven. Eternal life with God and all the souls and angels there. Heaven is the state of supreme and definitive happiness. It's the goal of the deepest longings of the human heart.

—Hell: The state of definitive—case-closed—self-exclusion from communion with God and the souls and angels in heaven.

It's for those who refuse, by their own free choice, to believe and be converted from sin, even to the end of their lives on earth.

—Purgatory: This is the state of final purification after death and before entrance into heaven. It's for those who have died in God's friendship but were only imperfectly purified. It's a final cleansing of human imperfection before one is able to enter the joy of heaven.

Heaven and hell are final, eternal destinations. The end of the line, everybody out. Purgatory is temporary. The next stop, guaranteed, is heaven.

You might not realize this, but the Church says something about what happens to your body, too. Your corpse isn't going to "stay dead." At some point in time, or, more correctly, at the end of time, Jesus will return to earth—the Second Coming. Bodies will be reunited with souls. (We'll get back to that in chapter 8.)

Your body will be reunited with *your* soul. Then, like Jesus now, you will have an incorruptible body. When the Catholic Church professes its belief in the "resurrection of the body" (to quote the Apostles' Creed) or "the resurrection of the dead" (as we say in the Nicene Creed), we don't mean just Jesus on Easter morning almost two thousand years ago.

We mean us. Each of us. We mean you: the body reading these words, the body that houses your soul. Sometime after the two have been separated by death and the soul enters heaven, hell or purgatory, both will be rejoined.

And live.

Forever.

Ever wish you could be immortal? *Ta da!* You are.

Here and Now Determines There and Then

How you live, what you believe, the choices you make, and the actions you take, determine where you will spend forever. That's worth repeating: *What you do in this life will affect what happens to you after you die.*

Why? Because the God who created you, the one who created everything, gave you free will. That means you get to decide what you're going to do and what you're not going to do. God made you because he loves you. Again, "you" being singular, an individual. He created you to love him.

But you don't have to. He's not going to twist your arm. You don't have to lead a moral life. You don't have to care about anyone else. You don't have to be a loving person if you don't want to be.

You don't even have to love *God*, if you don't want.

That doesn't mean he'll stop loving you, or that he'll take away your ability to choose. Even if that means you spend the rest of eternity separated from him.

How Can You Know for Sure
What Happens When You Die?

Still don't get it? None of us does. Not really. God is beyond our understanding. And the little we know about him is what he revealed to us humans about himself.

He began revelation in a particular way some 3,800 years ago when he chose an obscure fellow in an obscure place to establish a people. That was Abraham. His story can be found in the first book of the Bible, Genesis. (*Go to: "What's the Deal with ... Bible Stories?"*)

What's the Deal with ... Bible Stories?

Q: Are the stories in the Bible true?

Yes. And no. Some are literally true. What they describe actually happened. Others use a form of writing that tells a truth, but it isn't like a factual newspaper account.

Q: Why are there different styles?

We tend to think of the Bible as a single book, but it's more like a library. A collection of seventy-two books written by a number of authors over many centuries. Those authors were writing for different audiences.

Each was inspired by the Holy Spirit. Each was presenting God's revelation. That's why the Church says that, ultimately, God is the single author.

Q: Don't some Christian denominations believe all of the Bible is to be taken literally?

Yes, but Catholicism doesn't. It says that to understand the authors' intentions, the reader has to take into account the condition of each author's time, and the modes of feeling, speaking, and narrating then current. Some of the Bible is historical presentation. Other parts are prophetic and poetic texts. Still others use various forms of literary expression.

Q: How can the average reader know which is which?

By learning more about the Bible and getting help from a trustworthy teacher, book on Scripture, or translation with good introductions to each book and plenty of footnotes. Then it can be read and interpreted in the light of the same Spirit who inspired it.

Short version: God made a covenant (a deal) with Abraham. Abraham does this. God will do that. And part of the bargain was Abraham's descendents would be God's "Chosen People." The ones to whom he would reveal more about himself. The ones to whom he would one day send the Savior.

The Savior of the world.

Why did the world need saving? The same reason there is death today. Sin. (That's the topic of chapter 3.)

Then God *did* send that Savior: Jesus. And Jesus told us even more about our Father. Christ entrusted his teaching, this revelation, to his apostles. After the death of the last one, probably just before the end of the first century, public revelation ended. We humans had everything we needed to know, although it has taken us time to understand what we were taught. We're still figuring that out. (That's known as "the development of doctrine.")

One thing we know is we're the only earthly creatures who have free will. We are the only ones who can say "no" to God. We can give God the ultimate "no." He offers us heaven, but we can graciously, or not so graciously, decline.

Why? Because, as I said before, he loves us that much.

So we each decide where our souls will go after we die, where—ultimately—our souls will be reunited with our bodies. We are able to choose heaven because of Jesus. But we don't have to. Jesus never said, "Believe in me, or I'll punch your lights out."

The bishops put it this way in the Second Vatican Council document called *The Pastoral Constitution on the Church in the Modern World* (its Latin title is *Gaudium et Spes*—"Joy and Hope") in a section on the mystery of death:

It is in the face of death that the riddle of human existence grows most acute. Not only is man tormented by pain and by the advancing deterioration of his body, but even more so by a dread of perpetual extinction. He rightly follows the intuition of his heart when he abhors and repudiates the absolute ruin and total disappearance of his own person.

Man rebels against death because he bears in himself an eternal seed which cannot be reduced to sheer matter. All the endeavors of technology, though useful in the extreme, cannot calm his anxiety. For a prolongation of biological life is unable to satisfy that desire for a higher life which is inescapably lodged in his breast....

The Church ... firmly teaches that man has been created by God for a blissful purpose beyond the reach of earthly misery. In addition, that bodily death from which man would have been immune had he not sinned (cf. Wis 1:13; 2:23-24; Rom 5:21; 6:23; Jas 1:15) will be vanquished, according to the Christian faith, when man who was ruined by his own doing is restored to wholeness by an almighty and merciful Savior.

For God had called man and still calls him so that with his entire being he might be joined to him in an endless sharing of a divine life beyond all corruption. Christ won this victory when he rose to life, since by his death he freed man from death (cf. 1 Cor 15:56-57). Hence to every thoughtful man a solidly established faith provides the answer to his anxiety about what the future holds for him. At the same time, faith gives him the power to be united in Christ with his loved ones who have already been snatched away by death; faith arouses the hope they have found true life with God. (GS, 18)

Instant Replay

- You hate death because part of you wasn't made to die. (And it won't.)
- Science and medicine can prolong life, but existence in *this* life will always be far from perfect.
- You were made for something better.
- Your body wouldn't face death if we humans hadn't turned from God.
- Thanks to Jesus, your body won't stay dead. Your body and soul can be with God forever.
- Because of Jesus, we are united with our loved ones even in death. Faith lets us believe the souls of our dead loved ones are already enjoying heaven.

We All Grieve

Does that final point mean we shouldn't grieve when a loved one dies? Not at all. Even if our faith is strong, we *miss* that person who has been "snatched away by death." And we hurt because our fellow loved ones are hurting, too.

Surely no one ever had more faith than Jesus, who was God and human at the same time. He felt the same pain we feel. When St. John writes about the death of Jesus' friend Lazarus, he says, "Jesus wept" (Jn 11:35).

We can be happy a friend won an around-the-world cruise, but we'll still miss her while she's away. We could rejoice if a parent or grandparent, a sibling or child, was swept away to a magical and mystical kingdom where he would know nothing but complete happiness ... but we'd still be sad that he's no longer around. We'd still want to visit with him the way we had in the past. Still want to exchange a hug or share a laugh. Sit down at a meal together or simply be with one another.

Death, as we all know, ends that. For the rest of our life on earth. While it may seem to be a long time before we will be together again—two souls in heaven—it isn't really.

Here Today, Gone ...

That's a message we've all heard countless times. One we still tend to ignore.

How many members of the senior generation have remarked on how quickly the years have passed? They can't believe they're in their eighth, ninth or tenth decade. In many ways it seems to them that just yesterday they were youths.

Those who live long enough come to realize that, as the psalmist wrote, "As for mortals, their days are like grass; they flourish like a flower of the field; for the wind passes over it, and it is gone, and its place knows it no more" (Ps 103:15-16).

The same is true for us. Don't believe me? Tell me about your great-great-grandfather. Do you even know his name? You are his descendant. His flesh and blood. What do you know about him?

Probably nothing. Or next to nothing.

If you have descendants, your great-great-grandchild will know little or nothing about you. A name, a date, a faded photograph of some stranger wearing clothes from a previous century.

All those who knew you, not simply knew about you, will be

gone. Yes, you will continue to "live on" through a DNA chain but....

You are that grass. Here for a brief season and then gone.

And perhaps not here for even a full season. There's no guarantee you will live to see your eighth, ninth, or tenth decade. Death can be that thief in the night, coming when we least expect it. After all, if we expected the burglar, we would be prepared wouldn't we? That's the image Jesus used when he described his coming once again at the end of time (see Mt 24:43). "You must be ready," he said.

Ready to Die?

Be ready for death. Be ready for Jesus to come again at the end of time. How? First, by remembering that you're going to die. Second, by acknowledging you don't know when, where or how. And third, by living a life that concerns itself with what really matters.

What matters? You know the answer to that: Be selfish. What? Let me explain. What matters is amassing the best possible treasure for yourself. The greatest riches. The most happiness.

That doesn't mean money. That doesn't mean material goods. That doesn't mean power or fame. No. Think bigger than that. Be smarter than that. The money, the goods, the power, the fame could disappear at any time.

A bad investment, a lawsuit, a shift at corporate headquarters, bad PR, and it's gone. *Poof.*

No, Jesus said, instead "make purses for yourselves that do not wear out, an unfailing treasure in heaven, where no thief comes near and no moth destroys" (Lk 12:33).

On the most practical level, bottom-line economics, it makes more sense to invest in the ultimate Blue Chip. That's because—and you know this!—everything you see, everything you touch, everyone around you, and even you, yourself, will be gone someday. Someday, sooner than any of us think, whether that "sooner" is tomorrow or decades from now.

But you don't have to work at building a treasure in heaven if you don't want to. You're invited and you're encouraged, but you aren't forced. You are free to choose.

None of this means money, material goods, power and fame are bad, in themselves. They can't be. They're nothing more than tools or by-products. Tools and by-products that can be used for tremendous good. Or can be misused for tremendous ... let's say it: evil.

They are tools that easily convert into blinders. Into weapons. Into golden calves.

Jesus warned about that, too. Right after his comment on purses and heaven, he added: "For where your treasure is, there your heart will be also" (Lk 12:34).

If you fall in love with money, goods, power and fame, you'll only have your heart broken. They will leave you or, eventually, you will leave them. You are, after all, going to leave life.

Invest Now

Jesus is telling us we can avoid that heartache. And it's not simply—to put it crassly—that we're piling up assets in that Big Bank in the Sky. It's that we can have a foretaste of heaven on earth. Your heart is going to be where your treasure lies. If it lies in consumer goods, it will be in consumer goods. If it lies in figuring out and trying to do God's will, your heart will be there.

You decide. The clock is ticking.

As the *Catechism of the Catholic Church* reminds us, "death puts an end to human life as the time open to either accepting or rejecting the divine grace manifested in Christ" (1021).*

Death, it notes with stark simplicity, "is the end of earthly life" (1007).

We measure our lives by time, it continues, as we change and grow old. As with all living beings on earth, death seems like the normal end of life. Death lends urgency to our lives. Remembering our mortality helps us realize that "we have only a limited time in which to bring our lives to fulfillment: 'Remember also your Creator in the days of your youth, ... before the dust returns to the earth as it was, and the spirit returns to the God who gave it' [Eccl. 12:1,7]" (1007).

We'll examine that spirit—your soul—next.

Ten on Death

Death is the separation of soul and body.

—St. Ambrose (c. 340-397)

For no sooner do we begin to live in this dying body, than we begin to move ceaselessly toward death.

—St. Augustine (354-430)

To keep death daily before one's eyes.

—St. Benedict (c. 480-c. 547)

If we fear death before it comes, we shall conquer it when it comes.

—Pope St. Gregory the Great (c. 540-604)

Nothing is more certain than death, nothing more uncertain than its hour.

—St. Anselm (1033-1109)

Death makes equal the high and low.

—John Heywood (c. 1494-c. 1578)

Happy are they who, being always on their guard against death, find themselves ready to die.

—St. Francis de Sales (1567-1622)

As sure as death.

—Ben Jonson (1572-1637)

All human things are subject to decay,
And, when fate summons, monarchs must obey.

—John Dryden (1631-1700)

So death will come to fetch you? No, not death but God himself. Death is not the horrible specter we see represented in pictures. The catechism teaches that death is the separation of the soul from the body; that is all. I am not afraid of a separation which will unite me forever with God.

—St. Thérèse of Lisieux (1873-1897)

Chapter Two

Every Body's Got Soul

I wasn't there when my father died. After a series of health problems stretching back for years, he passed away at the age of eighty.

My mother, my four siblings and I had been with him that morning, keeping vigil. We all knew the end would be coming soon. Dad's condition had deteriorated noticeably, especially in his final days. I suppose we were as prepared as any family could be when the patriarch is on his deathbed. We were terribly sad because he would no longer be with us, but we knew that what was about to happen was inevitable.

Our faith assured us of what would happen to him, once he died. He was going to be much, much better off than he was right here and now. Still we grieved and consoled each other. Still we prayed and we waited.

In the final days of my father's life, there was no way to know if the end was going to come in minutes or days. We had already said our good-byes to Dad, who at this point was unconscious. So we agreed to take shifts for the bedside vigil at the nursing home. My brother and one of my sisters would remain with him, so the others could go home and get some rest.

About an hour after I got back home, my brother called. Our father was no longer on earth. During those sixty minutes I had been away, his soul had left his body.

I drove back to the nursing home, entered his room and there he was ... and wasn't. His body was still in the bed, not looking particularly peaceful but no longer in distress.

Where was he now? That was the question that popped into my mind time and again over the next several months. Where are you now, Dad?

It was apparent that he was more than his body. And at some point, at some instant, between being a living, breathing person and becoming a corpse, something had happened.

Soul and Culture

Long ago we humans figured out that a human person is more than a human body. According to Christian teaching, it's the soul that makes the difference. However, other religions also recognize the point in time when something happens and a person stops. Or leaves. A hull, a husk, is all that remains.

Defining death as the moment when the soul leaves the body is dandy, but what does it really mean? The body part is easy. We can see the body. Hear the body. Touch the body. If it's been too long between showers, smell the body. It's a body that sees, hears, touches and so on. But the soul ... that's a lot tougher.

It's hard to think about the soul, and the implications of having an immortal soul or a mortal soul, because so much of the discussion has to be abstract. Those of us not schooled in philosophy or theology have to hang on to our hats as words and concepts like *being* and *non-being, essence* and *form,* are bandied about. It's good to consider it all, though.

- Who says that the body has a soul?
- Why are there so many different theological and philosophical perspectives?

- Does my soul cease to exist after my body shuts down?
- If not, what happens to it? Is there an afterlife? Or is time here on earth all we get?

How a culture or religion defines *soul* shows a great deal about what those people believe. As my philosophy of body and soul changes, so does my worldview. Am I just passing through? If so, what's next? If there's something, is it good or bad? If there's more than one something next, how do I increase my chances of avoiding the bad something and attaining the good something?

What of me is going to that good or bad something? Not my body, apparently. Not right away. The body is still here. It's the ... what?... that goes ... where?

So ... What Is Soul?

In this chapter, let's start with the "what." We'll look at "where" in the next few chapters.

A dictionary tells us *soul* is a noun. OK so far. It's:

1. *The immaterial essence of an individual's life. Immaterial* means "not consisting of matter, spiritual." (This sense of the word fits better than the secondary definition of "unimportant" or "trifling.") *Essence* is a fundamental nature or quality.
2. *The spiritual principle that is embodied in human beings.*
3. *An active or essential part.* (So chocolate chips really are the soul of a chocolate chip cookie?)
4. *Man's moral and emotional nature.*
5. *A spiritual force.*

Maybe we should look in a dictionary of Catholic terms. So let's try two Catholic sources, one written and published before the Second Vatican Council and one after that meeting of the world's bishops in the early 1960s.

The 1958 edition of *A Catholic Dictionary* says a soul is the thinking principle; that by which we feel, know, will, and by which the body is animated. It's the root of all forms of vital activity. It is a substance or a being that exists per se (by, of, or in itself). It is simple and unextended (not made up of separate principles of any kind). It is spiritual, so its existence and, to some extent, its operations are independent of matter. It's immortal.

The soul is the substantial form of the body, different from the souls of plants or animals. A plant can't move by itself. An animal can't reason. *(Go to: "What's the Deal With ... Plants' and Animals' Souls?")*

Our Sunday Visitor's Catholic Encyclopedia offers this definition:

Together with the body, the soul constitutes the substantial unity of the human being. It is the immaterial, immortal, directly created principle that constitutes a particular individual as human.

The distinguishing feature of the human soul is that it is rational or intellective. The immortality of the soul arises from its simplicity or lack of composition: unlike material things, there are no components into which the human soul can break up. Incorruptibility is thus one reason for the soul's immortality. Another is that man evinces [shows] unlimited spiritual capacities. Thus, although the soul and the body are a substantial unity, the soul is intrinsically independent of matter both in being and its origins.

The soul endures after biological death.

Further, the soul cannot be generated out of material conditions. According to Christian teaching, each soul is directly created by God. Human identity is nonetheless constituted by the unity of soul and body. The relation of the soul to the body is not an instrumental one, but a real, substantial one.

What's the Deal With ...
Plants' and Animals' Souls?

Q: Do plants and animals and people all have souls?

Catholic teaching has said yes, all three do, because all are living. The three have different kinds of souls.

Q: What are they?

A plant's is called vegetative. An animal's is sensitive. And a human's is intellectual. Each is the root of vital activity in that particular form of life.

Q: Are there any similarities?

In a way, since the third (your soul) contains the other two virtually. Here that means "in essence," not in some video-game unreal way. And a sensitive soul contains the vegetative virtually.

Q: So is a plant or animal soul immortal?

No, the vegetative and sensitive souls are both simple but incomplete substances, incapable of existing apart from matter. Because of that, they're neither spiritual nor immortal.

Potted Plants and You

So, according to the first explanation, every living being has a soul, a form of life. A dandelion seed takes root, grows, blossoms and sends out more seeds, but it doesn't howl in pain when hit with a jet of weed killer. A dog grows from puppyhood to maturity and yelps when someone accidentally steps on its tail but doesn't reason things out. Yes, its behavior can be conditioned and, yes, it can have sharp instincts; but it's never going to chitchat about yesterday's weather or worry about the fact that someday it's going to die.

And the dandelion's "soul," that which keeps it living, doesn't survive when the plant dies. Ditto with the dog. Only *we* are different. Only *our* souls are different.

While the first two have a form of life, we have a higher form. We have the ability to reason and to choose. In all creation, in heaven and in the cosmos, you—a human being—are the only entity to be both matter and immortal spirit.

The weed and the dog have bodies—they have life—but not immortal souls. The angels of heaven are spirits only. No bodies. But when God created us, he put both together. And that's what makes us human.

Even before God stepped into our history in a particular way with Abraham and the Chosen People, even before he sent his Son (a human *and* God, which is beyond what the human mind can completely comprehend), we people had been thinking about this body-life, body-no-life business.

We had thought a lot about death because death has been a part of every people, every culture, every land.

And—because we are creatures who can reason and like to reason—we've tried to figure it out. Since we're creatures who can feel and do feel, we've tried to find comfort after the death of a loved one and find hope even as we realize that someday that will be our fate, too.

Since we are creatures who are both spirit and matter, our minds have turned toward our Creator, toward God, even when we could not name him. Even when our understanding of him was even more limited than it is now. (The only reason we know more now is because he has chosen to reveal more to us.)

Truth in Philosophy, World Religions ... and Scripture

Since the beginning of time, people have tried to tackle these "soulish" questions from a philosophical point of view. (At its Greek root, *philosophy* means "the love of wisdom.") Our Christian understanding has been influenced by Plato and Aristotle. That's not to say that what we believe is in some way "pagan," but what they reasoned contains some truth.

In the East, early Hinduism taught that the *atman,* the soul or self, was what controlled a person's activities and defined self-identity and consciousness. The *atman,* the Hindus said, could be identified with "Brahman," that is, with the divine, and that meant the soul had an eternal dimension. The soul, they said, is intricately linked to the body and in a cycle of reincarnation until it is purified and knowledgeable enough to merge once again with the ultimate reality.

One way Buddhism differs from Hinduism, and holds a unique spot in the history of major religions worldwide, is that it says the soul is an illusion created by a number of psychological and physiological influences.

In the West, the early Greek philosophers had no concept of a nonmaterial being. In other words, if something existed, it had to have physical properties. Plato (427-347 B.C.) is credited with coming up with an argument for an immaterial soul. Aristotle, his top student, picked up the ball from there and ran with it. Plato believed the soul was a pure spiritual principle, the subject of thought, distinct from the body and immortal. Aristotle said the soul unites with the body as a form united to matter. Yes, he said, the soul is the subject of thought, but its spirituality and its immortality aren't as evident.

Plato also held that souls were created from all eternity and so they existed before being joined to bodies. Among other non-Christian theories was the belief that souls existed from the beginning of time and passed from one body to another.

Scripture scholars point out that the word "soul" in English translations isn't a good choice for the Hebrew word *nepes*. Whether we know it or not, our concept of soul is based on that Greek/Christian understanding, and that wasn't the case in Old Testament times.

In the Old Testament, the *nepes* is different from the flesh (Dt 12:23) but not in the same way the spirit is. Sometimes the *nepes* has fleshlike experiences, suffering grief and pain, for example (Ps 42:5, 7).

The *nepes* leaves the body at death (Gen 35:18) but it doesn't continue as a living being. A "dead *nepes*"—which couldn't happen in Greek thought—is just a dead person (Lv 2:11). People pray for the deliverance of the *nepes* from Sheol, the underworld or abode of the dead (Ps 16:10). But those passages have to do with preserving one's life from death, not with calling forth a separate spiritual entity from the dead.

Human beings are *nepes* because, as described in Genesis 2:7, God breathed into Adam who then becomes a "living *nepes*." This wasn't the breath of life, it's something more. Even so, the Scripture scholars say, the association between *nepes* and life is so close, "life" is sometimes the best translation for the Hebrew term.

Nepes can also mean "self." One loves his neighbor as he loves his *nepes* (1 Sm 18:1). And it can mean "person." Or "anyone." It's also where the human appetites are centered, and when those appetites are satisfied, the *nepes* is full. It can mean even more.

So what is it? There is no single word in modern language that's its equivalent. A human, in his total essence, is a *nepes*. It is the self, concrete and existing. (Again, the ideas and explanations are abstract. They have to be.) Consciousness is life, the way the *nepes* is manifested.

Good for the Psyche

The Old Testament uses the Greek concept of soul (*psyche*) in only one book: Wisdom (3:1 and 8:19-20). When we read an English translation of the New Testament, then "soul" is the translation of that Greek word. However, that doesn't mean it was what the Greek philosophers meant by the word.

As in the Old Testament, the psyche is associated with life and it leaves the body at the time of death (Lk 12:20). Loving one's psyche is loving life (Rv 12:11). Paul says his psyche means nothing as long as he does God's will (Acts 20:24). In many ways, psyche is simply the equivalent of *nepes.*

There is a difference. The psyche is the seat of supernatural life. It's what is supernaturally saved. We can kill the body but not the psyche. God can do both (Mt 10:39). The loss of the psyche is so complete even inheriting the entire world would not compensate for it (Mt 16:26). The rest that Jesus offers the psyche isn't refreshment but the assurance of salvation (Mt 11:29). Disciples are to hate their own psyches (Lk 14:26); the one who wishes to save his psyche loses it, and the one who loses it for Christ's sake finds its and saves it (Mt 16:25). Why? Because what the world considers taking care of the psyche will destroy it. The self lives by saying no to the world and yes to Jesus (Jn 12:25).

Again, it's important to remember that psyche in the New Testament is not completely synonymous with the Platonic understanding of the term. However, it isn't something completely new and radical either. In the New Testament it is the total self, a living and conscious person. And the radical concept, is the meaning of life and salvation. Salvation offered to this *nepes-psyche*.

Middle-Aged Soul

In the Jewish world of Jesus' time there was no single teaching, or understanding, about eternal life. By the Middle Ages the soul was defined in Judaism as the principle of life, capable of surviving after biological death.

Islam has a similar teaching. According to the Koran, God breathed the soul into the first human beings and at death the souls of the faithful are brought near to God.

Among Christians, what Plato and Aristotle had taught, the line of thought they had begun, was later examined, addressed, built on and modified by St. Augustine, St. Thomas Aquinas and others. In Scholasticism—the Catholic theology and philosophy that developed in the Middle Ages— Plato's immortality and spirituality were united with Aristotle's conception of form.

Now Christianity may have a well-developed and relatively concise explanation of body and soul, life and death, but it didn't happen without some struggles. There were some mistakes, some heresies, that had their moments of popularity.

It's not hard to understand why. It was Aquinas, harkening back to Aristotle, who crystallized the idea of the soul and body as two distinguishable elements of a single substance. However, in earlier centuries, Christian thought struggled with the sometimes popular belief that the soul, somehow, was the prisoner of the body. That view could be a springboard to all sorts of widespread errors, including, for example, Gnosticism. One Gnostic belief was cosmological dualism: spirit (your soul) is in essence morally good while matter (your body) is in essence morally bad.

Church historians attribute the first Christian classic on psychology (the study of the psyche) to a treatise written by the theologian Tertullian in the third century. In *De Anima*, he points out that all philosophies fail to clearly show the nature of the soul and he argues that Christ alone can teach the truth about it. That's not to say he hit every nail on the head. He founded a theory called "Traducianism," from the Latin *ex traduce*, meaning "from the shoot of a vine." It said a human obtains a rational soul by procreation from the soul of the parent. That made it easier to explain original sin (which we'll look at in the next chapter).

The argument was that if the parents make the soul and their souls are tainted by original sin, the offspring's will be, too. For a time, it was the common theory in the West. It's handy and logical, but not accurate. Theologians discarded it a long time ago, in favor of Creationism. In this context, "Creationism" doesn't mean a belief in a literal interpretation of Genesis, God's making the cosmos in six twenty-four-hour days. Rather it refers to the belief that each individual human soul is created from nothing by God at the moment of conception or at least when the body is sufficiently formed.

Some said the infusion took place in the instant of conception of the fetus. Others—including Aristotle, St. Thomas and the Scholastics (up to the seventeenth century)—said it happened when the fetus had taken the organic human shape. They believed that the fetus had to be sufficiently developed to receive a soul.

Since then theologians have dropped Aquinas' opinion. That's a development of doctrine that parallels what science knows today about human life (genes, DNA and the rest) and when it begins.

Body and Soul Together:
Vatican II Insights

In the twentieth century, the bishops at Vatican II stressed "though made of body and soul, man is one." In *Gaudium et Spes* (14), they continue: "Through his bodily composition he gathers to himself the elements of the material world; thus they reach their crown through him, and through him raise their voice in the free praise of the Creator" (cf. Dn 3:57-90).

We humans are the height of God's material creation. Our very existence is a tribute to the One who made us.

"For this reason," the bishops immediately add, "man is not allowed to despise his bodily life; rather, he is obliged to regard his body as good and honorable since God has created it and will raise it up on the last day."

No Gnosticism allowed!

So, "when he recognizes in himself a spiritual and immortal soul, he is not being mocked by a fantasy born only of physical or social influences, but is rather laying hold of the proper truth of the matter" (GS, 14).

We humans don't come to believe in a soul—in something within us, that *is* us—that is more than material because we've been conditioned to believe it by society. Or taught to believe it by our religion or our culture. That ability to recognize we are more than our physical bodies is a part of our makeup.

The bishops put it this way:

Man judges rightly that by his intellect he surpasses the material universe, for he shares in the light of the divine mind. By relentlessly employing his talents through the ages, he has indeed made progress in the practical sciences and in technology, and the liberal arts. In our times he has won superlative victories, especially in his probing of the material world and in subjecting it to himself.

Still he has always searched for more penetrating truths, and finds them. For his intelligence is not confined to observable data alone, but can with genuine certitude attain to reality itself as knowable, though in consequence of sin that certitude is partly obscured and weakened. (GS 15)

Among the "penetrating truths" the Church teaches is the existence of the soul and its relation to the body. As the *Catechism of the Catholic Church* puts it: "The human person, created in the image of God, is a being at once corporeal and spiritual" (*CCC*, 362).

Body and spirit.

It adds that the biblical account expresses this reality in symbolic language when it says that "then the Lord God formed man of dust from the ground, and breathed into his nostrils the breath of life; and man became a living being" (Gn 2:7). "Man, whole and entire, is therefore *willed* by God" (*CCC*, 362).

Later, the *Catechism* explains that in Scripture the term "soul" often refers to human *life* or the entire human *person*. It also refers to the innermost aspect of that person, that which is of greatest value to him or her, that by which the person is most especially in God's image. "'Soul' signifies the *spiritual principle* in man" (*CCC*, 363).

It notes that the unity of both "is so profound that one has to consider the soul to be the 'form' of the body: i.e., it is because of its spiritual soul that the body made of matter becomes a living, human body; spirit and matter, in man, are not two natures united, but rather their union forms a single nature" (*CCC*, 365).

Further, the Church says every spiritual soul is created immediately by God—it's not "produced" by the parents—and also says that it's immortal. It doesn't die when it separates from the body at death, and it will be reunited with the body at the final Resurrection (*CCC*, 366).

So, to be honest, the opening lines of chapter 1 aren't entirely accurate.

There would be just as much truth in saying this:

You're never going to die.

You. Reading these words. You are never going to cease living. It's a done deal.

Ten on the Soul

The soul we define to be sprung from the breath of God, immortal, possessing body, having form, simple in its substance, intelligent in its own nature, developing its power in various ways, free in its determinations, subject to the changes of accident, in its faculties mutable, rational, supreme, endued [provided] with an instinct of presentiment, evolved out of one.

—Tertullian (c. 160-c. 222)

The life whereby we are joined unto the body is called the soul.

—St. Augustine (354-430)

For the soul is the inner face of man, by which we are known, that we may be regarded with love by our Maker.

—Pope St. Gregory the Great (c. 540-604)

It enjoys freedom and volition and energy, and is mutable, that is, it is given to change, because it is created.

—St. John Damascene (c. 675-c. 749)

Every soul is itself heaven in a sense—a heaven with understanding for its sun, faith for its moon, and virtues for its stars, a heaven where God dwells according to his faithful promise, *We will come to him and make our abode in him* [Jn 14:23].

—St. Bernard (c. 1090-1153)

God is the life of the soul—as the efficient cause, not the formal cause.

—St. Thomas Aquinas (1225-74)

I began to think of the soul as it were a castle made of a single diamond or of very clear crystal, in which there are many rooms, just as in heaven there are many mansions.

—St. Teresa of Avila (1515-82)

And, when life's sweet fable ends,
Soul and body part like friends:—
No quarrels, murmurs, no delay;
A kiss, a sigh, and so away.

—Richard Crashaw (1612-49)

The greatness of the soul is her capacity to love.

—Archbishop William Bernard Ullathorne (1806-89)

Souls are like athletes, that need opponents worthy of them, if they are to be tried and extended and pushed to the full use of their powers, and rewarded according to their capacity.

—Thomas Merton (1915-68)

Chapter Three

Sin: Enter Trouble With a Capital T

Being in the second grade meant receiving my First Holy Communion. This solemn (and no doubt stress-filled) rite of passage occurred on Mother's Day, 1960. It began with First Confession on Saturday.

First Confession was very serious business, even for a seven-year-old. Or maybe especially for a seven-year-old. "Bless me, Father, for I have sinned," we were instructed to begin. "This is my *first* confession."

Sister emphasized the word. After that initial encounter, each of us would say how long it had been since the last one. "These are my sins," each of us was to continue.

And then came the list.

So, on the evening before, I grabbed a thick blue pencil and a Big Chief tablet and prepared to write my list. I knew I couldn't take it into the box with me. Even if I did, I wouldn't be able to decipher it in the dark. But jotting it all down seemed to be a clever idea.

Not so, my mother gently told me when she found out my plan. My sins, it seems, were between God and me and the priest sitting there *in persona Christi,* "in the person of Christ." When he said, "I absolve you," it was Jesus saying those words.

Forgiveness is so personal, I would later realize, because sin is so personal. Even the misdeeds of a second-grader, as minor as they might be, were a private matter. (As I grew older, it occurred to me that Mom was also sparing me the embarrassment of having that list fall into the hands of curious siblings, some of whom would have been only too happy to add items that had apparently slipped my mind.)

I don't remember what I told the priest the next day. It's easy to imagine. A cookie stolen here. A spat with my brother there. It was, though I didn't realize it at the time, the story of humanity, writ small. It was "salvation history," engraved on the head of a pin.

The "Big Picture" of Salvation

The same story—larger, bolder, more colorful—is what the Old and New Testaments offer. That's so because the entire Bible can be summed up in two words:

1. Sin (the subject of this chapter).
2. Redemption (the subject of the next one).

Scripture scholars point out that there is no single Hebrew word with theological overtones comparable to our *sin*.

That's not to say there isn't sin in Scripture. It's chock full of the idea, from the get-go, because the Bible's a recounting of human history (and divine intervention). But when the writers of the Old Testament talk of "sin," they use a number of different words with a number of different connotations.

Hatta (or *het'*) is a common one. It means "to miss the mark." This word signifies not just an error in judgment but a failure to attain a goal. It was also used to indicate the breaking of an agreement between nations or peoples. It could be disloyalty between a lord and his servant. Or it could include failure to fulfill one's obligation as a host. It didn't necessarily mean *doing* something, rather, it could be *not doing* something.

The Hebrew word *awon* is often translated as "iniquity," which means wickedness. It emphasizes a failure or distortion. Reality has become what it ought not to have become. The sinner has created wickedness by his or her act. Hand in hand with that new reality is guilt, a burden that can be incredibly heavy for the sinner to bear. This word also conveys the reality of sin's consequences; our wrongdoing has not only offended God, but has also caused us to stray from the path that leads to our true destination. In the truest sense, we have become lost in our sins.

Still other Hebrew words—all translated into English as "sin"—have to do with rebellion. A child against her parents. A citizen against someone higher up politically. An Israelite against Yahweh. Again, in this context "sin" signifies the breaking of a covenant or an agreement. It's a personal offense. It's an act that stirs up anger and leads to the sinner hating Yahweh.

There's more. Words for "sin" also suggest disorder, evilness and ugliness, being twisted or bent out of proper form. Sin is an abomination—meaning something disgusting or loathsome. Sin is a lie. That doesn't mean just the particular sin of telling an untruth but every sin is an attempt to deceive by pretending to be something that it is not. It denies reality, by action or speech. All sin is foolishness.

Where Did Sin Originate?

Where did sin come from? Scripture scholars say this question needs to be considered both psychologically and historically, beginning with the Old Testament.

Psychologically, sin comes from the lack of knowledge of God: a person refuses to know, to accept, Yahweh—refuses to recognize God's reality. Sin comes from an evil heart. Sin is a deliberate and willful act. Sin breaks down society.

Historically, sin goes back to the first humans' decision to disobey God. They had free will. They chose how to act. Our first parents may have been tempted by someone outside themselves (Satan, and we'll look at him in chapter 6), but it was within their power to resist. Instead, they gave in because they wanted to be something they were not.

The first act of disobedience severed the relationship between humans and God. We now call that act "original sin." (We'll get to that a bit later in this chapter.) It didn't completely cut those ties, but the damage wasn't something mere mortals could repair. Paradise was lost until Yahweh sent the Savior.

Yes, in each age God punishes sin, but his punishment is tempered by mercy. Even so, by sinning, humanity has condemned itself. Genesis 3 shows the result of sin is this self-inflicted curse. And it's the same thing with every sin. This isn't God's fault. Humanity chose sin and, by doing so, chose death. In the Old Testament, there is no evil—no personal or societal disaster or affliction—that is not attributed to sin. And, in the thinking of the time, that is simple justice.

The Original Top Ten

The writers of the New Testament, and the early Christian community, had the same concept of sin. Scripture scholars say it can be classified in three general categories:

—A single act.
—A state or condition.
—A power.

As we'll examine more closely in the next chapter, it is Jesus, the Redeemer, who conquers sin's power on every front.

Among the words for sin in the New Testament are the Greek *hamartia, anomia* and *adikia. Harmatia* is comparable to the Hebrew *hatta.* Again, missing the mark, it's tossing aside the ways God intended us humans to live.

Anomia—anarchy or lawlessness—hammers home the point that to sin is a rebellion against God and his laws.

Adikia, or injustice, stresses that sinning is our saying "no" to a life in the justice God offers us.

Sin is also *skotos* (darkness) and *pseudos* (falsehood)—preferring those to the Light and the Truth.

St. Augustine summed it up nicely in the fifth century: "All sin is a kind of lying." (That's from his work titled "On Lying.") It is a betrayal of what a person is. Who a person is.

The Israelites came to understand this because Yahweh presented a straightforward contract: the Ten Commandments. (*Go to: "What's the Deal With ... the Ten Commandments?"*) There was the whole arrangement, in broad strokes. Over time, the Chosen People came to understand how they could be applied. How they were to be lived in any situation, under any circumstances.

It wasn't just Yahweh and Israel—the people—who had a contract. It was Yahweh and each individual Israelite.

But as anyone who has ever followed a set of rules or written a set of policies knows, those items can be bent into incredible shapes. They can be used in ways that, it seems to anyone with any sense, are pretty much the opposite of the purposes for which they were first written.

In the Hebrew world, it was the Pharisees who knew the law well. Not just the Big Ten but the seemingly countless major, minor and minuscule clauses that were developed from them. That's not a bad thing. How could it be bad to know how to apply the Ten Commandments? No, where they got off the track was in *not* applying them. A Pharisaical-based law or interpretation of the law could be a handy loophole for them.

Equally scandalous, they—truth be told, like all of us—had the ability to get high and mighty about the minutia and completely ignore the spirit of the law. And they could be hypocritical, not practicing what they preached. "Whitewashed tombs," so bright on the outside but full of decay within (see Mt 23:27-28).

Accentuate the Positive

But that was then, right? And since Christ came, we who follow him ...

Miss the forest for the trees, as well. We need the Ten Commandments. We need to know right from wrong. We need to know what is and what isn't sinful. And yet, we often fail to see that the Commandments weren't created to fence us in, but to set us free.

Why? Because they and we have the same Maker. We weren't created to ignore him. We weren't created to turn our backs on our earthly parents. We weren't created to kill one another, to sleep around, to steal, to lie, to be immobilized and seethe with anger because someone has something we don't. We weren't created to worship a "golden calf," no matter what form it might take. (Money, power, fame, stuff.)

We're better than that. All those sins are missing the mark, are lies, because that's not why we were created. Acting that way hobbles us. It keeps us from becoming what we were meant to be. Who we were meant to be.

Jesus knew all this, of course. He knew that those who had a covenant with God then, and those who have one with him now, can have a hard time with "don't" and "can't." If we focus too much on the negative, then the absence of negative seems like a positive.

"Hey, I didn't *kill* anyone, OK?"

But that isn't always the case. As the Pharisees proved.

So Jesus, referring to two Old Testament passages, gave the people the two "greatest commandments":

—Love God with your whole heart, soul and mind.

—Love your neighbor as you love yourself. (See Mt 22:34-40, Dt 6:5 and Lv 19:18.)

And he offered the Beatitudes (see Mt 5:1-11) which, not surprisingly, fit hand in glove with the Ten Commandments. Not that they are a perfect mirror image, but that they are a simple list of "do's" rather than "don'ts."

Blessed are ... The poor in spirit. Those who mourn. The meek. Those who hunger and thirst for righteousness. The merciful. The pure in heart. The peacemakers. "Blessed" doesn't mean "holy" in the sense of wimpy or overly pious. Another translation, perhaps a better one, is "happy."

If you live this way, you will be happy. If you follow the Commandments, you will be happy. That doesn't mean you won't have hard times, that you won't experience true sorrow.

This "happy" means a deep joy, a profound peace, based on a spiritual foundation. Based on a personal and unique relationship with the Father, Son and Holy Spirit. And it's that relationship for which each of us was created.

For which you were created.

You were made by God to be with God. By following the Commandments (to look at it from a negative point of view) and living the Beatitudes (the positive slant) you nurture that relationship. How so? They allow you to become "more human." More the creature—the being made up of body and soul—God intended you to be.

Sin 1.0

God knows, God really knows, we each fall short of the mark. Every human being has, and everyone will. Except two. Jesus and his mother, Mary. The Church teaches that the Blessed Mother (and Jesus, of course) was conceived without original sin.

What is that sin? The *Catechism* says the story of the fall in Genesis 3 uses "figurative language but affirms a primeval event" (390), a deed that took place at the beginning of human history. "Revelation gives us the certainty of faith that the whole of human history is marked by the original fault freely committed by our first parents" (390) (Cf. Council of Trent: DS 1513; Pius XII: DS 3897; Paul VI: AAS 58 (1966), 654).

After that first turning away from God, the world was flooded with sin. And because of that first sin, our human nature is weakened. It's subject to ignorance, suffering and the domination of death. And it's inclined to sin.

Just as sin was a hot topic in the Old and New Testaments, it continued to be in the early writings of the Church. Sometimes it was a list of don'ts. Sometimes it was a collection of dos.

"Didache" was a summary of teachings and practices at the end of the first century. "There are two ways," it begins, "one of life and one of death." It then goes on to offer a Commandments/Beatitudes combination. "The way of life, then, is this: First you shall love God who made you; second, your neighbor as yourself."

Applying Jesus' teaching—and his radical approach to behavior—it continues: "Bless them that curse you, and pray for your enemies, and fast for them that persecute you. For what thanks is there if you love them that love you? Do not the Gentiles do the same? Love those that hate you and you shall not have an enemy."

The sin, then, isn't just what can be seen on the outside. Rather, as Jesus taught, it's what happens on the inside. When we sin, we are those whitewashed tombs. Sin leads to death. Not our physical demise. We all face that, saints and sinners alike. But the end of "us." The end of the "me" God created me to be. And, again, becoming that "me" is the only way I can truly be happy.

St. Augustine put it this way in *The City of God:* Sin is "a revolt against God." It is "love of oneself even to contempt of God."

All the Same but Different

To be honest, sin can be tricky. Not just because we can be tempted by Satan, just as our first parents were. But because an action that is sinful for one person might not be a sin (or as great a sin) for someone else. How is that possible?

The *Catechism of the Catholic Church* explains that sin is an offense against reason, truth and right conscience (1850). Due to our "perverse" attachment to certain things, we fail to genuinely love God and neighbor. This is contrary to eternal law, as noted by both St. Augustine and St. Thomas Aquinas.*

So every sin is basically the same but that doesn't mean all sins are identical.

St. Paul listed some specifics in his letter to the Galatians

---

*What is "eternal law"? It's the source, in God, of all law (*CCC,* 1952). Sin sets itself against God's love for us and it turns our hearts away from it.

(5:19-21): fornication, impurity, licentiousness, idolatry, sorcery, enmities, strife, jealousy, anger, quarrels, dissensions, factions, envy, drunkenness, carousing, and the like.

"I am warning you," he wrote, "as I warned you before; those who do such things will not inherit the kingdom of God."

But, again, this isn't limited to a list of "don'ts." The apostle goes on to point out "by contrast, the fruits of the Spirit" in verses 22 and 23. They are love, joy, peace, patience, kindness, generosity, faithfulness, gentleness and self-control.

Types of Sin

But St. Paul's first list is, to a large degree, "sins of the flesh." They aren't, by any means, the only kinds of sin. Each of us can be very creative when it comes to sinning, but every sin can be categorized. All sins can be "distinguished according to their object, as can every human act," the *Catechism* explains (1853). Or, it adds, they can be pigeonholed according to the virtues they oppose or the commandments they violate.

They can be classified according to whether they concern God, our neighbor or ourselves. (All of them ultimately concern all three, of course.) Whether they are spiritual or carnal. Whether they are sins in thought, word, deed or omission. (As the Confiteor at Mass puts it: "In what I have done and in what I have failed to do.")

Why do we have the potential to become such stellar sinners? It goes back to our free will. That marvelous God-given gift that allows us the complete freedom to choose the Giver. Or not.

We can pick love or its opposite, which is more than simply hate. We can commit big sins or little ones.

What's the difference in "size"? That's a major classification the Church uses. Every sin, it teaches, is either mortal (deadly) or venial (capable of being forgiven). That doesn't mean mortal sins are unforgivable. It refers to *how* we can obtain that forgiveness.

The teaching that there are those two basic categories has its foundation in Scripture. "All wrongdoing is sin, but there is sin that is not mortal" (1 Jn 5:17). That belief became a part of the tradition of the Church.

Deadly Sins

Our doctrine says mortal sin "destroys charity in the heart of man by a grave violation of God's law" (*CCC,* 1855). It turns a person away from God, who is everyone's ultimate end and "his beatitude"—his true happiness—"by preferring an inferior good" to God.

On the other hand, venial sin "allows charity to subsist, even though it offends and wounds it."

Let's look at mortal sin first. Because it attacks the vital principle within us—charity—we need "a new initiative of God's mercy and a conversion of heart which is normally accomplished within the setting of the sacrament of reconciliation" (*CCC,* 1856).

Three Conditions of Mortal Sin

1. *Its object is a grave matter.* That's spelled out in the Ten Commandments. The gravity of a sin can be more or less. Murder is graver than theft. Abusing one's parents is graver than abusing a stranger.
2. *It's committed with full knowledge.* The sinner has to know it's a sinful act.
3. *It is done with deliberate consent.* The sinner makes that choice. Pretending ignorance about its wrongness or having "hardness of heart" increases, rather than decreases, the voluntary character of the sin. However, if you really don't know something is wrong, "unintentional ignorance" can lessen or even remove the "imputability of a grave offense" (*CCC*, 1860).

If I know it's a sin and do it anyway, I've sinned. If I don't know it's a sin and I do it, I haven't sinned.

At the same time, no one can claim "I didn't know" for every sin because no human (of sound mind) can be considered ignorant of the principles of moral law. These, the *Catechism* says, "are written in the conscience of every man" (1860).

There can be other extenuating circumstances. Promptings of feelings and passions can lessen the voluntary character of the act. So can external pressures and pathological disorders.

By the same token, a sin committed through malice, one committed by deliberately choosing evil, is the gravest.

Again, we're capable of something so awful because we're capable of picking something even more wonderful. We can choose love. We can choose God. But when we commit that grave sin, that mortal sin, we lose that charity within us. We deprive ourselves of "sanctifying grace." (We'll talk about that in the next chapter.) If it isn't given back to us by God—by our repentance and God's forgiveness—we exclude ourselves from Christ's kingdom and choose hell. (We'll examine hell in chapter 6.)

We have the freedom to make that choice and not turn back. But even though we can judge that an act in itself is a grave offense, "we must entrust judgment of persons to the justice and mercy of God" (*CCC*, 1861).

Our "Teeny-Tiny Sins"

A venial sin is committed when the matter is less serious and we don't observe what's prescribed by the moral law. Or it's when we disobey the moral law in a grave matter but we do that without full knowledge or complete consent.

Of course, even "smaller" sins take a toll. They weaken our ability to love. They show a disordered love of things. They hinder our soul's ability to practice the virtues and what is morally good. And they "merit temporal punishment" (*CCC*, 1863). (We'll examine that in chapter 7.)

Then, too, they dispose "us little by little to commit mortal sin" (*CCC*, 1863).

And, as Pope John Paul II pointed out in *Reconciliatio et Paenitentia* (Reconciliation and penance): "Venial sin does not deprive the sinner of sanctifying grace, friendship with God, charity and, consequently eternal happiness."

The *Catechism* quotes St. Augustine:

While he is in the flesh, man cannot help but have at least some light sins. But do not despise these sins which we call "light": if you take them for light when you weigh them, tremble when you count them. A number of light objects make a great mass; a number of drops fills a river; a number of grains makes a heap. What then is our hope? Above all, confession.

From *"In Epistulam Johannis ad Parthos Tractatus"*—
"Tractates on the First Letter of John"

So even "little sins"—over time and through repetition—can harden our hearts. They can create an inclination toward sin. As sin builds on sin, our conscience becomes less reliable and our judgment skewed. Like a cancer, sin can quickly reproduce itself and become stronger. But it cannot destroy the core of morality that is in each of us.

The Sins of Society

The *Catechism* makes one final point in its section on sin. When we cooperate in the sins of others, we have a responsibility for those acts. That's the case if we take part directly and freely; if we offer our advice, praise or approval or if we order them; if we fail to disclose them or fail to hinder them when we have an obligation to do so; and when we offer protection to those committing evil acts.

We can't use as our defense that we're the three monkeys who hear no evil, see no evil, speak no evil. We don't remain blameless because we refuse to hear, refuse to see, refuse to speak. That's because sin can be part of an institution or a social situation. There can be structures of sin that we have an obligation to address or we bear part of the responsibility for their existence. Racism is a good example. So is abortion.

We can't—like a self-declared neutral country in the middle of a world war—claim this has nothing to do with us. We can't wring our hands and lament living in a "sinful world" and do nothing to stop that sin, even when what we do seems so meager.

Sin doesn't ever have to win, because sin has already been conquered. In the next chapter, we'll look at how that was done and what it means for each of us.

What's the Deal With ...
the Ten Commandments?

Q: Where did we get the Ten Commandments?
That list comes from the book of Exodus, chapter 20, verses 2-17. God gave them to Moses on Mount Sinai. The Decalogue (a Greek word meaning "ten words") can also be found in Deuteronomy 5:6-21.

Q: What was happening when Moses received the Commandments?
The Israelites had fled Egypt, where they were slaves, and were still on their way to the Promised Land. Exodus tells the story of their journey.

Q: Why are they so important?
They list our fundamental duties toward God and neighbor. Those duties are never going to change. They are part of the covenant—the agreement—between God and humans.

Q: Did the coming of the Messiah make them obsolete?
Not at all. Jesus taught that the Decalogue has to be interpreted in light of the "great commandment" of love of God and neighbor (see Mt 22:34-40).

Ten on Sin and Sinners

Sin ... is a fearful evil, but not incurable; fearful for him who clings to it, but easy of cure for him who by repentance puts it from him.

—St. Cyril of Jerusalem (c. 315-86)

The end of sin is death.

—St. Basil (c. 329-79)

Prosperous sinners fare worst of all in the end.

—St. John Chrysostom (c. 347-407)

Everyone who commits sin is the slave of sin.

—St. Ambrose (c. 340-97)

Sin is nothing else than to neglect eternal things, and seek after temporal things.

—St. Augustine (354-430)

Sin becomes much more scandalous when the sinner is honored for his position.

—Pope St. Gregory the Great (c. 540-604)

The body of a sinner is a tomb, covering a soul dead by sin.

—St. Thomas Aquinas (1225-74)

Since the goodness of God is so great that one single moment suffices to obtain and receive his grace, what assurances can we have that a man who was a sinner yesterday is so today?

—St. Francis de Sales (1567-1622)

There are only two sorts of men: the one the just, who believe themselves sinners; the other sinners, who believe themselves just.

—Blaise Pascal (1623-1662)

To be a sinner is our distress, but to know it is our hope.

—Archbishop Fulton J. Sheen (1895-1979)

Chapter Four

Redemption and Grace
(Thank God)

Our oldest child was in seventh grade when my wife Monica and I switched roles. She headed out to finish getting her degree in social welfare and go to work in that field. I stayed home to freelance write and take care of the kids.

That fall Tom made the wrestling team, and I washed his brand-new uniform (red) in the same load with his brand-new wrestling shoes (white).

Oops.

No matter how many times I sent the shoes through again, no matter how much bleach I used, I could still see pink. He could still see pink. Anyone who looked closely could still see pink.

It's tough to be a macho seventh-grade wrestler in pink shoes.

In salvation history, humanity faced a similar dilemma. Once brand-new and spotless, we became permanently marked with the stain of sin. No matter what we did, the stain remained—both on us and on all creation.

We needed help. We needed redemption.

And Ransom Captive Israel

In the Old Testament the Hebrew words for "redeem" and "ransom" can mean the same as our English words. Something is paid for someone's release. Sometimes "redemption" is simply a metaphor. Yahweh didn't offer Pharaoh cash to free the Israelites from slavery in Egypt. Rather, he used his power. And the Lord also redeems with his love.

To be redeemed could mean to be freed from distress or trouble, or from an enemy. In the early Scripture, the Chosen People could be redeemed either individually or as a group. Which was a good thing; as we saw in chapter 3, it wasn't just the Israelites as a nation that could sin by breaking their covenant with God, but each individual person, too.

Ransom, New Testament Style

The New Testament writers use "ransom" in similar ways but they also talk of avenging and atoning. While the Old Testament focuses more on redemption as being released after a price is paid, the New emphasizes liberation.

Jesus liberates not just by paying the ransom but by *being* the ransom. "The Son of man came not to be served but to serve, and to give his life as a ransom for many" (Mt 20:28). He does this voluntarily. He does it not for himself but for others.

To whom is the ransom paid? To God? To Satan? Both those ideas were examined by the Church Fathers, those early Christian theologians. As it turns out, neither is precisely accurate.

Our sins had set the human race off track. By breaking the

covenant, we had created realities far from what God intended for us. The ransom Jesus paid for us frees us from our sins and all their consequences.

That's something we just couldn't do for ourselves. And although forgiveness is something God grants to us readily, Scripture scholars point out, "The ease with which it is granted may mislead one concerning the tremendous work which was done to establish it" (from *The Dictionary of the Bible* by John L. McKenzie, S.J.).

The ransom—the death of Christ—is the highest price ever paid for anything. Now forgiveness is readily attainable because it came at such a great cost. Jesus is both God and human. It's in his human nature that he suffers and dies for us but the one who suffers and dies—at the same time—is God.

Because he is God, Jesus is able to take our place, is able to take onto himself the unimaginable burden of the world's guilt. So though Jesus himself never sinned, he suffers more from sin than any other human being ever has—or ever will. He suffers more because he is totally undeserving of it. He suffers more because he knows the Father so intimately and realizes what it means to be without him, to have lost him forever.

We can't ever truly comprehend that pain because we can't ever truly comprehend the relationship of the Three Persons in the Blessed Trinity. Why was the Second Person the one to become a human? In his excellent book *Theology for Beginners*, F.J. Sheed explains: "Creation as a work of omnipotence, bringing something into existence of nothing is appropriated to God the Father. But the order of the universe, as a work of wisdom, is appropriated to the Son. The order had been wrecked, and a new order must be made; it was the Son who made it."

Every Sunday

But then that's common knowledge. Or it should be. At every Sunday Mass when we pray the Nicene Creed, we say: "For us men and for our salvation he came down from heaven; by the power of the Holy Spirit, he was born of the Virgin Mary, and became man."

And we add: "For our sake he was crucified under Pontius Pilate; he suffered, died, and was buried."

For us. For our salvation. For our sake.

Jesus, already and always the Second Person of the Blessed Trinity, became a human being to save us by reconciling us with God. This wasn't like some fine we owed God because of sin. It wasn't some debt with a loan rate so high we could never do more than scrape together the monthly interest charge. The world was out of whack. We humans had done that. And we could continue to do it. There was no way we could fix it. Which is a very good indication of just how serious and how powerful sin is.

In a work titled *Oratio Catechetica*, the fourth-century theologian St. Gregory of Nyssa put it this way:

Sick, our nature demanded to be healed; fallen, to be raised up; dead, to rise again. We had lost possession of the good; it was necessary for it to be given back to us. Closed in the darkness, it was necessary to bring us the light; captives, we awaited a Savior; prisoners, help; slaves, a liberator....

Are these things minor or insignificant? Did they not move God to descend to human nature and visit it since humanity was in so miserable and unhappy a state?

Jesus became a human because "God's love was revealed among us in this way: God sent his only Son into the world so that we might live through him. In this is love, not that we loved God but that he loved us and sent his Son to be the atoning sacrifice for our sins" (1 Jn 4:9-10).

Jesus became a human to act as a model of holiness for us. We are to follow his way. To act as he acted. To love as he loved.

Amazingly enough, Jesus became a human to make us "participants of the divine nature" (2 Pt 1:4). In his *Opusculum*, St. Thomas Aquinas explained: "The only-begotten Son of God, wanting to make us sharers in his divinity, assumed our nature."

So, to use another metaphor, this redemption Jesus brought didn't just get us out of the hole we had dug for ourselves. It set us on a mountaintop.

The Good News

That's the Good News. That's the "Paschal mystery." Jesus died on the cross and rose from the dead. God's plan for salvation was accomplished "once for all" (Heb 9:26). And even though, since that first sin, God had promised to save humanity from its errors, even though the Chosen People had entered a covenant with Yahweh and anxiously awaited the coming of the Messiah, the Anointed One wasn't recognized by all.

Just the opposite. Some declared Jesus a blasphemer, one who threatened the tenuous relationship between the Israelites and the foreign power that occupied their land, the Romans.

Others realized Jesus was a teacher, a rabbi, who spoke with authority. And while his words were backed with powerful actions—with miracles—some found his declarations to be just too much. Jesus was over the top. Jesus was just too far out there. Urging his followers to "eat my flesh," for example. (See Jn 6:51-58.)

The Gospels tell how Judas, on his own, betrayed Jesus. How the Messiah was handed over by the Jews to the Romans and tortured and put to death. Sadly, for too long the Christian spin on this was that the Jews were responsible for the crucifixion. Jews, of any age, were "Christ killers." (*Go to: "What's the Deal With ... the Crucifixion?"*)

But that's not true. The Jews didn't kill Jesus.

You did.

You, reading these words.

I did.

I, writing them.

Salvation wasn't just for "humanity," that seemingly infinite lump of people of all time. The Second Person of the Blessed Trinity became a human being for each of us, individually. For you. For me.

Although he was God, he accepted being mocked. Being tortured. Being nailed to the cross. Dying the extremely painful and humiliating death of a prisoner.

Although he was God, he accepted that his mother, Mary, would see everything that happened to her son, her little boy.

He endured it all for you because he loves you that much. He endured it all because none of us—wallowing in our own sins and the consequences of the sins of others—could find our way to the Father except through him. He is the way. He is the truth. He is the life. (See Jn 14:6.)

Redemption isn't abstract. It isn't historical. It is right here, right now. It is Jesus and you. It is Jesus and me.

Like our first parents, we should run and hide in shame when

God approaches. How, in justice, could we expect anything but the most severe punishment possible for the sins that put his only Son on the cross?

Think of all this in simply human terms. Your child, the flesh of your flesh, is dragged out and beaten to death. Now the one who committed the unspeakable act stands before you. You have the authority to determine his or her fate.

And because Jesus' two natures—human and divine—can't be separated, his death was even worse than that. To what can we compare the execution of the Second Person of the Blessed Trinity? A human killing another human is a terrible thing to ponder. But creature killing his Creator? Unthinkable.

God's Mysterious Plan

God continually surprises us. Time and again, his love leaves us dumbfounded. Though we are fully deserving of the worst possible punishment, separating us eternally from God, we receive only his mercy. Our God doesn't punish us because of our sins. He offers us his Son in our place.

This was God's mysterious plan for salvation. He will demonstrate the opposite of sin, he will show us true love, and in doing so will heap upon himself the pain, the isolation, the guilt of all sins—of every sin that has been committed or will be committed.

Of your every sin.

Of mine.

Jesus' death was no accident. It didn't just happen. As St. Peter explains in his first sermon on Pentecost, Christ was "handed over ... according to the definite plan and foreknowledge of God" (Acts 2:23). This doesn't mean Judas, Pilate and the others were robots or zombies. Although God already knew what their choices would be, they freely chose them. This isn't predestination. God—who created time, who is outside time—already knows our choices, too, even as he gives us the free will to make up our own mind and act.

However, it wasn't as if God hadn't tipped his hand before Jesus arrived. Through his prophets, he foretold his plan. His "servant," "the righteous one" was going to "make many righteous" and "bear their iniquities" (Is 53:11). He "poured out himself to death, and was numbered with the transgressors" and "bore the sin of many, and made intercession for transgressors" (Is 53:12).

And it wasn't as if Jesus hadn't told people the same thing. (As we already mentioned in this chapter: "The son of man came ... to give his life as a ransom for many.") Even after his Resurrection, he hammered home that point. "Was it not necessary that the Messiah should suffer these things and then enter into his glory?" (Lk 24:26). And then, when his followers still weren't too clear on all this, "Beginning with Moses, he interpreted to them the things about himself in all the scriptures" (Lk 24:27).

Paul got the message and passed it on: "Christ died for our sins in accordance with the scripture" (1 Cor 15:3). It's a theme, a teaching, he came back to time and again.

Unfortunately, because some of those passages are so familiar to us, they lose a lot of their punch. Or we never really stop to listen to the words and consider the message. But if we start to pay attention, that recurring theme—God's plan—can be plainly seen. And three points become clear:

First, Jesus did all this although he was blameless.

Second, we did nothing to deserve being saved.

And third, he did it for each one of us.

The *Catechism of the Catholic Church* quotes the Council of Quiercy (in what is now France): "There is not, never has been, and never will be a single human being for whom Christ did not suffer" (*CCC*, 605) (Council of Quiercy (853): DS 624; cf. 2 Cor 5:15; 1 Jn 2:2).

A Contract Signed in Blood

The *Catechism* also points out that at the Last Supper, when he instituted the Eucharist, Jesus anticipated the offering he was going to make the next day. He gave his apostles—he gives us—his body and his blood. He offers them for the forgiveness of sins. This is the New Covenant, the new agreement, between God and humanity. It is founded on, rooted in, Jesus' passion and death.

Jesus freely and lovingly makes this sacrifice which "completes and surpasses all other sacrifices" (*CCC*, 614) (Cf. Heb 10:10). How so? It's a gift from God the Father. The Father handed his Son over to sinners to "reconcile us with himself" (*CCC*, 614). And, at the same time, it's an offering of the Son of God made man, who offered his life "to his Father through the Holy Spirit in reparation for our disobedience" (*CCC*, 614) (Cf. Jn 10:17-18; 15:13; Heb 9:14; 1 Jn 4:10).

The *Catechism* tells readers that the Council of Trent emphasized the unique character of Jesus' sacrifice as the source of our salvation and it taught that his death on the cross "merited justification for us" (*CCC*, 617) (Council of Trent, DS 1529).

Justification by Faith

That final term is one that might ring a bell. *Justification* was one of the flash points during the Protestant Reformation.

In everyday language, to "justify" something means to prove it's just, right or reasonable. (We can justify leaving work early Friday afternoon because we had to stay late on Thursday.) It also means to pronounce free from guilt or blame. Or to adjust or arrange exactly.

In theological language, *Our Sunday Visitor's Catholic Almanac* defines it this way: "The act by which God makes a person just, and the consequent change in the spiritual status of a person, from sin to grace; the remission of sin and the infusion of sanctifying grace through the merits of Christ and the action of the Holy Spirit."

The *Catechism* says: "The grace of the Holy Spirit has the power to justify us, that is, to cleanse us from our sins and to communicate to us 'the righteousness of God through faith in Jesus Christ' and through Baptism [Rom 3:22; cf. 6:3-4]" (*CCC*, 1987).

See the problem? The paradox? How can we square Jesus' cleansing us completely from our sin, from our guilt, when we continue to sin? We continue to be guilty. And if he has redeemed us—which he has—then how can we claim we play any role in that happening? Isn't that more than a bit ... presumptuous?

Taken to what might be considered its logical conclusion, aren't we saying Jesus didn't quite get the job done and it's up to each of us to mop up?

No. But it's easy to misinterpret or misapply what the Church does teach. It's easy to understand why Martin Luther's "justification by faith" struck a chord. It's only in our own time, more than four centuries after Luther and the Council of Trent, that the heat that controversy generated has subsided enough for both denominations to examine what the other has said and recognize there is common truth in each.

More than a millennium before Luther, the Church was arguing against the other extreme. A heresy known as Pelagianism denied the necessity of grace for salvation.

How we are saved—justified—is important because it shows that we have a role to play in it. That obligation extends beyond ourselves. We play a part, or can choose to play a part, in redemption.

This all goes back to Scripture, of course, and especially St. Paul's writing which speaks of justification by faith. (See Rom 8 and Gal 3.) That's balanced by James, which notes "a person is justified by works and not by faith alone" (2:24). And "just as the body without the spirit is dead, so faith without works is also dead" (2:26).

How Does It Work?

So, going back to the *Catechism of the Catholic Church*, just *how* does the Holy Spirit do this? How does he cleanse us from our sins? How does he communicate the righteousness of God through faith in Jesus Christ and through baptism?

That happens, the *Catechism* says, because through the Holy Spirit's power we—right here, right now—take part in Jesus' passion by dying to sin. And we take part in his Resurrection by being born to new life. We are members of his body, that is, the Church. We are "branches grafted onto the vine which is himself" (*CCC*, 1988) (cf. 1 Cor 12; Jn 15:1-4).

But what are the steps in that process? The stages we go through? The *Catechism* says the Holy Spirit's first work of grace is conversion. Jesus told the people to repent because the kingdom of heaven was at hand (Mt 4:7). So, "moved by grace, man turns toward God and away from sin, thus accepting forgiveness and righteousness from on high" (*CCC,* 1989).

Quoting the Council of Trent, the *Catechism* adds: "'Justification is not only the remission of sins, but also the sanctification and renewal of the interior man'" (*CCC,* 1989) [Council of Trent (1547); DS 1528].

So justification detaches us from sin, "which contradicts the love of God" and purifies our hearts of sin (*CCC,* 1990). It follows God's offers of forgiveness. It reconciles us with him. It frees us from "the enslavement to sin" and it heals us (*CCC,* 1990).

Simultaneously, it's *"the acceptance of God's righteousness* through faith in Jesus Christ" (*CCC,* 1991). ("Righteousness" means the rectitude—or virtue, goodness or morality—of his love.) With that righteousness, the theological virtues of faith, hope and charity "are poured into our hearts, and obedience to the divine will is granted us" (*CCC,* 1991).

This is available to us, "has been *merited for us,*" by Christ's suffering and death (*CCC,* 1992). It's conferred in the sacrament of baptism and "conforms us to the righteousness of God, who makes us inwardly just by the power of his mercy" (*CCC,* 1992).

Its purpose is "the glory of God and of Christ, and the gift of eternal life" (*CCC,* 1992) [cf. Council of Trent (1547); DS 1529].

So, once we're baptized we lose our free will and become Christian automatons? No, not at all. "Justification establishes *cooperation between God's grace and man's freedom*" (*CCC,* 1993).

We Still Have a Choice

In other words, God justifies us with us. In his *Summa Theologica*, St. Thomas Aquinas explained: "The sinner is justified by God moving him to righteousness; 'it is God that justifies the ungodly' (Romans 4:5). Now God moves all things according to the mode of each.... In those who can exercise their free will the motion from God to righteousness is not without a motion of free will; he infuses justifying grace in such a way that he moves at the same time the free will to accept the gift" (I-2, 113, 3).

In simple terms, through the grace of God we more clearly see what is better for us. Obviously, that *is* God and his plan for us. But even though we see it we are not forced to choose it. Rather, the wisdom of the Holy Spirit—that Spirit that is Wisdom—helps us realize it would be foolish, even tragic, to choose other than God.

However, we have to make a choice. Even if we fail to decide and act, that *is* a choice we make.

Because of Christ's passion and death, because the spotless Lamb of God was sacrificed for our sakes, we can avoid being fooled by sins' smoke and mirrors. And, what's also amazing, we can join our own suffering, our private Way of the Cross, to Christ's to help not only ourselves but others.

Our generous God lets *us* play a role in redemption. Suffering is and always has been a consequence of evil, of sin. But, and this is important, that's not to say those who suffer are evil or sinful. Rather, suffering exists in this world because sin exists in this world.

As Pope John Paul II taught in his 1984 apostolic letter, *Salvifici Doloris* ("On the Christian Meaning of Human Suffering"):

The Redeemer suffered in place of man and for man. Every man has *his own share in the Redemption*. Each one is also *called to share in that suffering* through which the Redemption was accomplished. He is called to share in that suffering through which all human suffering has also been redeemed. In bringing about the Redemption through suffering, Christ *has also raised human suffering to the level of the Redemption*. Thus each man, in his suffering, can also become a sharer in the redemptive suffering of Christ.... (19)

If one becomes a sharer in the sufferings of Christ, this happens because Christ *has opened his suffering to man*, because he himself in his redemptive suffering has become, in a certain sense, a sharer in all human sufferings. Man, discovering through faith the redemptive suffering of Christ, also discovers in it his own sufferings; he *rediscovers them, through faith*, enriched with a new content and new meaning.... (20)

Does this mean that the Redemption achieved by Christ is not complete? No. It only means that the Redemption, accomplished through satisfactory love, *remains always open to all love* expressed in *human suffering*. (24)

Each of us can help pay that ransom and as we do, we can receive even more faith, hope and love to see even more clearly. Freed from sin, we can choose God. That's so important because the choices we make here and now affect our destiny forever.

God offers his sanctifying—his healing and saving—grace to help us become holy, to help us become more like him. More "in his image," which is, after all, how he created us.

That grace—that gift which makes the soul holy—is so critical because where and how we spend eternity depend on it.

What's the Deal With ... the Crucifixion?

Q: Why did Jesus die on a cross?

His death itself was for our salvation. The particular method of execution was the one used by Rome.

Q: Why did the Jews use a Roman method?

They didn't. First-century Palestine was under Roman rule.

Q: Was Jesus the only person ever crucified?

No. Even on Good Friday, two others were killed alongside him. Crucifixion was common throughout the Roman Empire from about the sixth century B.C. until Constantine banned it in A.D. 337.

Q: Why did the Romans use it?

It was extremely painful for the victim. Death took a while. And it was a powerful deterrent for anyone thinking about committing a similar crime.

Q: What crime did Jesus commit?

That's what the Roman governor, Pilate, wanted to know. The Jewish leaders had condemned him because he "blasphemed" by saying he was the Son of God. But Pilate, wanting to calm down a screaming mob, caved in and said, "OK, I'll order his execution but it's your fault, not mine."

Even one of his fellow condemned prisoners realized Jesus had committed no crime. Officially, the bogus charges were "perverting our nation, forbidding us to pay taxes to the emperor, and saying that he himself is the Messiah, the king"(Lk 23:2).

Ten on Redemption and Grace

No one is redeemed except through unmerited mercy.
—St. Augustine (354-430)

But if he had not himself undertaken a death not due to him, he would never have freed us from one that was justly due to us.
—Pope St. Gregory the Great (c. 540-604)

Christ ... gave himself.
—St. Thomas Aquinas (1225-74)

Every holy thought is the gift of God, the inspiration of God, the grace of God.
—St. Ambrose (c. 340-97)

Let grace be the beginning, grace the consummation, grace the crown.
—St. Bede the Venerable (c. 673-735)

He rideth at ease, that is carried by the grace of God.
—Thomas à Kempis (c. 1379-1471)

When God calls anyone to Christianity he obliges himself to furnish him with all that is required for being a good Christian.
—St. Francis de Sales (1567-1622)

A little reed in the hand of grace becomes a mighty staff.
—Bishop Jean Pierre Camus (1582-1652)

The burden of life is from ourselves, its lightness from the grace of Christ and the love of God.

> —Archbishop William Ullathorne (1806-89)

I have been groping in darkness, seeking where Thou wast not, and I have Thee not. But, O Lord my God, *Thou hast found me*—leave me not.

> —Father Isaac T. Hecker, C.S.P. (1819-88)

Chapter Five

Heaven: The Never-Ending Welcome-Home Party

Like most new parents with a house full of little kids, at one point in my life I would have defined heaven as half an hour of peace and quiet. Yes, I dearly loved Tom, Carrie and Andy, but just thirty minutes, please.

Or a little extra shut-eye. A Saturday morning when both Monica and I could sleep in without the children awake and on the *go!* at the crack of dawn.

Or a few extra dollars in my wallet. A trip to the grocery store without keeping track of every penny spent.

Like most seasoned parents whose children have grown up and moved away, at one point in my life I would have defined heaven as one more session of rough-and-tumble with those little ones.

Or the excitement of a Saturday family outing that started early and lasted late.

Or three very good reasons to spend those few more dollars renting the latest cartoon video.

That's the thing about heaven. It's the whole enchilada. Here on earth, at best, something is great but something is missing. What we have now is wonderful but what we had back then was pretty terrific, too. Why can't we have both at the same time?

It hardly needs to be said, but: Life on earth is not heaven.

And we have to forget all that heavenly hype about floating on clouds, getting fitted for wings and halo, and strumming a harp. We have to realize heaven isn't like some never-ending prayer service in a church without padded pews. It isn't being surrounded by an endless sea of those holier-than-thou folks who can be such a pain on earth. God has something much better planned for us.

What the Jews and Early Christians Believed About Heaven

If heaven isn't all those things—and thank God it isn't—what is it? And how do we know for sure? Did someone come from heaven to give us the inside scoop?

Actually, someone—Jesus—did just that. But even before he "came down from heaven" (as we pray in the Nicene Creed), we humans knew a thing or two about it. How? God told us, of course. Divine revelation. That's why any exploration of heaven needs to start with an examination of how it was presented in the Old Testament.

In those books, heaven is regarded both as a natural place and a theological idea. Physically, the Hebrews said, the universe was divided into three parts: the heavens, the earth and the abyss of water under the earth (or *Sheol*). When they spoke of "the heavens and the earth," they meant the visible universe.

The heavens were a half-circle vault over the earth, a big bowl or tent or a building resting on columns. There were windows through which rain fell. And storehouses with snow, hail and water. Yahweh brought those things out when needed.

God lived in heaven, though he was also present in earthly sanctuaries like the ark of the covenant and the temple in Jerusalem.

The prophet Elijah was taken up to heaven (2 Kgs 2:11). At the end of time the heavens would collapse and a new heaven and earth would be created (see Is 34:4; 65:17).

Jewish literature spoke of a number of heavens or stages, including "paradise," the garden in which humanity began.

In the New Testament, the kingdom of God is sometimes called the kingdom of heaven because of the Jewish practice of not saying or writing God's name. The New Testament also says Jesus was taken up into heaven (his Ascension), and at the end of time he will return from there (see Mt 24:30).

Scripture scholars point out that the heaven of the Old Testament was invisible and unattainable for all except Elijah. The heaven of the New Testament is the dwelling place and reward for those who follow Christ. God is building a home for us there (see 2 Cor 5:1-5). Our inheritance (see 1 Pt 1:4), reward (see Mt 5:12) and treasure (see Mt 6:20) are there.

Christ is the first to have a heavenly body, a resurrected body, but all those in heaven will be given heavenly bodies one day. Bodies that are incorruptible, glorious, powerful and spiritual (see 1 Col 15:42-49). (We'll look at that in chapter 8.)

What Heaven Is and What It Isn't

OK, but what *is* heaven? Really. And, also important, why would *I* want it?

"Heaven is the ultimate end and fulfillment of the deepest human longings, the state of supreme, definitive happiness," the *Catechism of the Catholic Church* says (1024).

Any foreshadowing of it, any "taste" of it on earth, is incomplete. Being the parent of those little kids was absolutely wonderful but.... Having raised them brings immense personal satisfaction but....

Whatever we have, whatever we do, on earth, it just isn't enough. This doesn't mean accumulating possessions or building up power or attaining worldwide fame—all tools which could be good or bad depending on how we use them. This means the goodness that comes from listening to God's will and following it. We can poke our noses into that kingdom of God while we're on earth (that kingdom which is here among us [see Lk 17:20-21]), but not enter it fully. Not in this life.

At the same time, entering fully is what we truly want. Even if we don't know it. That emptiness we feel inside—sometimes a lot of empty, sometimes only a little—is our wanting to be with God completely. And we can't be with him that way here and now.

Even when we experience those moments when our happiness seems almost complete, we know they soon will be over. That's not being pessimistic but realistic. It's only on soap operas that characters say with great conviction, "Now we'll be happy forever," only to have some calamity hit them in the face before the week is out.

There's another term the Church uses for heaven: "the beatific vision." *Beatific* means "great joy." It's seeing God, face to face.

Sort of.

The problem is heaven is beyond our imagining, so we have

no words to describe it. (It's *more* than what we describe as face to face.) And the descriptions we have traditionally used aren't necessarily the best or most accurate choices, going back to clouds and wings and such.

Heaven's Not on a Map

As Pope John Paul II has pointed out, it would be better to think of heaven as a state of being, rather than simply a location. Heaven "is not an abstraction, not a physical place amid the clouds, but a living and personal relationship with the Holy Trinity." So being in heaven isn't like being in Omaha or being in Tokyo. Being is heaven is like being in love.

But, with our meager minds, we don't know how to completely express that and so we fall back on symbolic language. Heaven—because it is so wonderful—is up there. It's above us. (Just as when we fall in love we say we're "floating on cloud nine.")

Since Jesus' resurrected body is bathed in glorious brightness and splendor, artists gave him a halo. Since the saints share in that, the painters gave them the same. Or maybe smaller ones.

What about us? Will we really have halos and wings? Angels—God's messengers—are shown with both. Some folks reason that, since we will be with the angels (or they incorrectly assume we will *become* angels after dying), we'll be given those "headlights" and handy limbs, too.

The same goes for harps. They were among the instruments used in the temple. Again, the popular tradition has said angels have them. So we will, too, someday. Right? And long white gowns, of course.

All this would make sense, of course—except for the fact that angels are angels, and humans are humans. (*Go to: "What's the Deal With ... Angels?"*)

We're No Angels

OK, those are some of the things heaven *isn't*. But what *is* it? Why would anyone, why would you, want this beatific vision? Because, if you don't want *it*, you don't want to go to heaven, right? And how do we see God face to face if, being bodiless souls, we don't have faces? And God, being God, doesn't have one either, except as the second person of the Blessed Trinity, Jesus.

Again, we use the words we can easily understand, the images that make sense to us, for an experience that is beyond our understanding. We won't know what heaven is really like before we actually reach heaven because we can't know, we are incapable of knowing that until we get to heaven.

Our limits have been compared to trying to explain red to a man born blind. Or a major chord to one deaf since birth. We can use many words to describe it but the individual cannot experience it. At best, it's a shadowy glimmer or a faint vibration.

We're like preschoolers who haven't learned to count yet who are trying to fathom calculus. Like little ones fumbling our way through the alphabet trying to decipher Plato's *Republic*.

Supreme Being, eternity and perfection are simply beyond us. Put all three together and....

Some times in our life may be great, they may be almost perfect. We may even exaggerate a bit and call them perfect. A perfect meal. A perfect afternoon. A perfect vacation.

But we know they aren't. They are very, very good. But

that's not perfect. Perfect is flawless. Right now and always. Our "perfect" meal may up our cholesterol level. The "perfect" afternoon may mean we're behind in work. The "perfect" vacation may leave us deeper in debt. Then, too, the meal, the afternoon, the vacation end.

What God offers us in the next life *is* perfect. "This perfect life with the Most Holy Trinity—this communion of life and love with the Trinity, with the Virgin Mary, the angels and all the blessed—is called 'heaven'" (*CCC*, 1024).

It's being with the One who created us, the One who made us to someday be completely happy with him forever. For eternity. The One who never began, who always is, created you to be with him forever.

Too Good *and* True

Why? What's the catch here? What's the fine print say?

No catch. No fine print.

God did that because he loves you. That's why he offers you the opportunity to share in his perfection.

And just when an idea, a divine revelation seems untoppable, God tops it. We can call this Supreme Being "Father." In the prayer that Jesus taught his disciples, the one we say at every Mass, we begin with the phrase "Our Father who art in heaven" (see Mt 6:9-15).

Again, this doesn't mean heaven is up in the clouds or that God is distant. It doesn't mean that the Great Clockmaker wound up the universe and then sat back to let whatever happened happen. As the *Catechism* explains, "who art in heaven" doesn't mean a place—a space—but a way of being. It doesn't mean that God is distant, but "majestic." Our Father is not "elsewhere." He transcends everything we can conceive of his holiness. It's precisely because he is so holy that he is "so close to the humble and contrite heart" (*CCC*, 2794).

It goes on to say that the symbol of the heavens refers us back to the mystery of the covenant we're living. He's in heaven. His dwelling place. That house is our homeland. Sin exiled us from it, but conversion of heart enables us to return.

How was this—is this—done?

"In Christ, then, heaven and earth are reconciled, for the Son alone 'descended from heaven' and causes us to ascend there with him, by his Cross, Resurrection, and Ascension" (*CCC*, 2795) (Cf. Isa 45:8; Ps 85:12) (Jn 3:13; 12:32; 14:2-3; 16:28; 20:17; Eph 4:9-10; Heb 1:3; 2:13).

Because all this is for everyone, it's easy to forget it's personal, too. It's you. Singular.

In heaven, you will not be absorbed into God or into all the other souls there and lose your identity, as in some science fiction movie. You will retain, or rather find, your true identity, your own name (*CCC*, 1025, cf. Rev 2:17). You—body and soul—are an individual, unlike any other that has been created or will be created. In heaven you will remain that unique "you" and come to see the true you God created you to be.

You will see others as they truly are, too.

O When the Saints ...

All the souls already in heaven are "saints," whether they are canonized or not. Together with the angels, the souls in heaven and in purgatory and the faithful on earth form the Communion of Saints. This group, which we can be a part of right now, can pray to and pray for one another for spiritual help.

The difference between the three (sometimes called the Church Triumphant, the Church Suffering and the Church Militant) is that the saints have died in a state of sanctifying grace or have been purified in purgatory. (We'll talk more about that in chapter 7.) The souls still in purgatory are being prepared for heaven. And those of us still on earth—us folks with body and soul together ...

Well, that's the heart of it, isn't it? If God created us, God redeemed us, God sustains us and God wants us to be with him forever, how do we get there?

Getting Past the Pearly Gates

If heaven is all the Church says it is, and the Church readily admits it's more than the Church could ever say, then how do we get past those pearly gates? How do we convince St. Peter to let us walk in and dance along those golden streets?

Gates of pearls and streets of gold are just popular images, of course. But, in a sense, St. Peter is the gatekeeper. Or, rather, the Church is. Because it's through the Church, in the Church, that the sacraments are celebrated. "Whatever you bind on earth will be bound in heaven, and whatever you loose on earth will be loosed in heaven" (Mt 18:18).

The Vatican II document *Lumen Gentium* notes that "bishops, as successors of the apostles, receive from the Lord, to whom was given all power in heaven and earth, the missions to teach all nations and to preach the Gospel to every creature, so that all men may attain salvation by faith, Baptism and the fulfillment of the commandments" (24).

So there is a fundamental relationship between the Church and getting to heaven. Not a membership card, but access to the sacraments that bring grace. Sanctifying grace is your ticket to heaven. No one enters without it.

Grace is what heals our human nature, which has been wounded by sin. It's what gives us a share in the divine life of the Trinity. The grace of Christ is the free gift that God makes to us of his own life, "infused by the Holy Spirit into our soul to heal it of sin and to sanctify it," the *Catechism* says (1999). "It is the *sanctifying* or *deifying grace* received in Baptism. It is in us the source of the work of sanctification" (cf. Jn 4:14; 7:38-39).

It's sanctifying grace, a habitual gift, a stable and a supernatural disposition that perfects your soul itself to enable you to live with God, to act by his love. "Habitual grace" means the permanent disposition to live and act in keeping with God's will, God's call for you.

Without that grace, without that gift freely given, we are incapable of heaven. We lack the ability to "see" God. We just can't do it.

"No Non-Catholics Allowed"?

But that brings up some questions, some concerns. If baptism is the key to obtaining sanctifying grace, and it is, then what if someone dies without being baptized? What about an infant? What about someone who never heard of Jesus? What about the Catholic who has renounced his faith, has ignored God's call and has committed serious sins? What about the Christian who just sort of let it all slide?

The *Catechism* is careful to point out that it was the Lord himself who affirmed that baptism was necessary for salvation. "Very truly, I tell you, no one can see the kingdom of God without being born from above" (Jn 3:5). It's the Church's obligation, its mission, to tell the world about the salvation offered through Jesus. To tell each person.

But suppose those missionaries never come to my town. I'm a decent person. I die. And then ... I don't get to go to heaven? No. Baptism is necessary for salvation if the Gospel has been proclaimed to you and you had the possibility of asking for that sacrament. But ... the *Catechism* adds: *"God has bound salvation to the sacrament of Baptism, but he himself is not bound by his sacraments"* (*CCC*, 1257).

That's why those who suffer death for the sake of the faith without having been baptized are baptized by their death for and with Christ. This "Baptism of blood, like the *desire for Baptism*, brings about the fruits of Baptism without being a sacrament" (*CCC*, 1258).

And every person who is ignorant of the Gospel and the Church but seeks the truth and does the will of God as he understands it, can be saved. We can suppose that such persons would have *"desired Baptism explicitly* if they had known its necessity" (*CCC*, 1260).

What if someone is baptized in another denomination? The Church says there is only one baptism. That act changes the soul. It leaves an "indelible mark." So someone can't be re-baptized if she wants to enter the Catholic Church. Instead she would make a profession of faith. (That's what happens at the Easter vigil Mass. Those who were never baptized receive the sacrament. Those who were, profess their faith in the Catholic Church.)

And Then There's Limbo

But what about babies? What about "limbo"? That word came from the Latin *limbus,* meaning "border" or "edge," as in the edge of hell. Some early theologians thought that would be the place for souls without any sin except "original sin."

Later, most Catholic writers accepted that explanation, but the Church never declared it an official teaching. The *Catechism* says nothing about it by name. But it notes: "As regards *children who have died without Baptism,* the Church can only entrust them to the mercy of God, as she does in her funeral rites for them" (1261).

An all-loving God is going to take good care of these precious little ones.

How Do We Know?

It's important to keep in mind that Jesus didn't dictate all this to his apostles, giving them everything just as we have it today. Rather, what we know about limbo—about death, the soul, sin, redemption, grace, heaven, purgatory, hell and final judgment— is part of the "development of doctrine."

In this context, the "doctrine" of the Catholic Church is all the teachings in faith and morals given to the Church by Christ through the apostles for the sake of our salvation. It's what Jesus taught and told the apostles to teach us. This is called "revelation."

Public divine revelation ended with the death of the last apostle. Right from the start, the Church has had all the doctrine revealed by Christ. But (and this is a very important "but"), we humans can't necessarily understand all that it contains or its practical consequences. Guided by the Holy Spirit, we can "get" more of it. Over time.

The message, the teaching, remains the same. Our understanding of it can deepen, and the changes in society—both good and bad—can mean that doctrine has to be applied in new ways.

Maybe a better way of saying this is that the development of doctrine means we develop in our understanding of that doctrine.

That's why, for instance, missionaries in the past worked so feverishly to have as many people as possible baptized. In previous centuries, baptism alone—in one form or another—was seen as the way to salvation. It's why St. Monica prayed so diligently—and nagged her boy so relentlessly—that her son Augustine be baptized. The belief, the fear, was that any loved one who had not received the waters of baptism stood no chance of gaining heaven.

Even in our own time, a common pre-Vatican II concept was that anyone not baptized in the Catholic Church could not enter heaven. More than one youngster scurried home from parochial school or CCD (religious education) class deeply concerned that a non-Catholic parent or grandparent would be doomed.

The Church's doctrine developed, too, as it began to address the question of those who were baptized but then renounced the faith to save their necks from Roman persecution and then, later, wanted back into the fold. Or those who were duly baptized and who never officially left the Church, but were notorious sinners. Baptism wiped out their sins, but what about those new ones? These people couldn't be rebaptized.

The answer of course is the sacrament of reconciliation (or penance or confession). None of this means it's impossible for someone to actually go to hell. We'll examine creation's "hot spot" in the next chapter.

What's the Deal With ... Angels?

Q: *What are angels?*
Spiritual creatures that serve God in heaven and as messengers on earth. They "continually see the face of my [Jesus'] Father in heaven" (Mt 18:10) and are "mighty ones who do his [God's] bidding, obedient to his spoken word" (Ps 103:20).

Q: *How do we know angels exist?*
Scripture and Tradition. That is, what the Bible says and what the Church has always taught.

Q: *Why do we call these beings "angels"?*
The word comes from the Greek *angelos*, meaning "messenger." In Scripture God often used angels as his messengers.

Q: *So they're like robots?*
No. They have intelligence and will. Like us. They are personal (one angel is different from another) and immortal. They surpass in perfection all visible creatures. (That is, us.)

Q: *How old are the angels?*
They have been present since creation.

Q: *How many angels are there?*
There are exactly ... we don't know.

Q: *What is the relationship between devils and angels?*
We'll talk about that in the next chapter.

Q: *What's a "guardian angel"?*
Human life, from its beginning until death, is surrounded by angels' watchful care and intercession.

St. Basil (c. 329-379) wrote: "Beside each believer stands an angel as protector and shepherd leading him to life" (Adversus Eunomium III, 1: PG 29, 256B).

Q: *So I have a special angel "assigned" to me?*

Yes! A powerful friend is always with you, ready to help you. The Church celebrates your angel's feast day on October 2.

Ten on Heaven

Eternal life is the actual knowledge of truth.

—St. Augustine (354-430)

To desire eternal life with all spiritual longing.

—St. Benedict (c. 480-547)

God now appears as he wishes, not as he is. No wise man, no saint, no prophet is able to see him as he is, nor has been able in this mortal body.

—St. Bernard (1090-1153)

Nobody is excluded from the kingdom of heaven except through human fault.

—St. Thomas Aquinas (c. 1225-74)

What does heaven mean for a rational soul? Nothing else than Jesus, God.

—Walter Hilton (d. 1395)

For a small living men run a great way, for eternal life many will scarce move a single foot from the ground.

—Thomas à Kempis (c. 1379-1471)

The world is only peopled to people heaven.

—St. Francis de Sales (1567-1622)

O happy harbor of the saints,
O sweet and pleasant soil;
In thee no sorrow may be found,
No grief, no care, no toil.

In thee no sickness may be seen,
No hurt, no ache, no sore;
There is no death, nor ugly devil,
There is life evermore.

—Anonymous, "Jerusalem, My Happy Home"
(sixteenth century)

Earth has no sorrow that heaven cannot heal.

—St. Thomas More (1779-1852)

Love of heaven is the only way to heaven.

-Cardinal John Henry Newman (1801-90)

Chapter Six

Hell's Bells ... and Whistles

Heaven sounds like a wonderful idea. At the same time, many folks would like to believe hell simply doesn't exist. After all, they reason, how could this all-merciful and all-loving God send some soul down to the fiery pit forever?

The answer is a lot like an eighth-grade civics class. I remember mine. I was classroom president, which seemed like a great honor until I found out it included running a meeting every Friday afternoon.

Civics class was the reason for it. The educational theory was that while learning about democracy in our society, we were experiencing it in the classroom. We, this group of some thirty students would be the ones determining ... what?

Not much.

For instance, we could never vote for a free day. Never decide to have pizza delivered for lunch. Never abolish tests or grades. No, we—always strictly following parliamentary procedure—could open the meeting, have the minutes read and approved, consider old business, discuss new business and vote on closing the meeting.

Any decision, any issue, was always within the strict and clear limits set by our teacher. Simply put, we didn't have free will.

Which brings us back to hell. So to speak.

Free will is what God gives us. That's why life is not like an eighth-grade civics class. It would be if there were no hell.

Think about it. If God acted like an eighth-grade teacher and said, "You can decide but only within this very limited range," then we wouldn't really have the ability to choose. But what he gives us is the maximum.

"You, my dear little creations," he says to us, "are free to accept me or not. I will never force myself on you. If you want nothing to do with me, you can have nothing to do with me. I made you to be with me forever. But you can choose to be without me forever."

Without him forever. That's hell.

How *Gehenna* Got Its Name

How do we know about hell? The same way we know about heaven. Scripture and Tradition. Divine revelation.

As mentioned in the previous chapter, in the Old Testament the opposite of the heavens was *Sheol*, the underworld, the place of the dead. What we could consider hell was Gehenna, a name that came from "valley of the son of Hinnom." Scripture scholars speculate he was the original owner of a piece of land just outside Jerusalem, a valley that separated the ancient city from the hills to the south and west.

It was known as an unholy place because, at one time, it had a cultic shrine where human beings were sacrificed. Kids. The prophet Jeremiah cursed it and predicted it would be a place of death and corruption (Jer 7:32; 19:6 ff). It was called a spot for the bodies of those who rebelled against Yahweh, a place of never-ending fire and physical corruption.

Over time, the word came to mean the place of eternal punishment. In the New Testament, Gehenna is a place of unquenchable fire (Mt 5:22; Mk 9:43), a pit into which people are cast (Mt 5:29). It's where the wicked are destroyed (Mt 10:28). Sinners are punished in this fire prepared for the devil and his fellow demons (Mt 8:18).

The New Testament says Gehenna is like a prison or a torture chamber (Mt 5:25-26). A place of misery where there is weeping and gnashing of teeth (Mt 8:12). A place of darkness where the worms continue to eat away at the rotting body (Mk 9:48; Mt 8:12).

All those images were common in first-century Jewish literature, biblical and otherwise. But when the New Testament writers' audiences were Gentile-Christians rather than Jewish-Christians, the authors talked about God's anger as he punished the sinner (Jn 3:8; 5:24 ff). It was exclusion from the eternal life talked about by Jesus (Jn 5:29). It was darkness (Jn 8:12). It was death (Rom 6:23). It was not sharing in the kingdom of God (1 Cor 6:10). It was eternal destruction (Phil 3:19; 2 Thes 1:9).

These images, Scripture scholars point out, are just that: images. They aren't to be taken literally. What is certain is judgment, followed by eternal reward or punishment. But just as we relatively feeble-minded human beings can't begin to grasp what heaven is, we can't clearly define and understand hell.

We can say hell is worse than anything we know. We can say it is the opposite of what we truly want. Ultimately, hell is God honoring our request that he get lost. Hell is being left alone, continuing an existence without his presence, choosing to be excluded from it.

John Paul II on Hell

In a weekly general audience in the summer of 1999, Pope John Paul II put it this way:

God is the infinitely good and merciful Father. But man, called to respond to him freely, can unfortunately choose to reject his love and forgiveness once and for all, thus separating himself forever from joyful communion with him. It is precisely this tragic situation that Christian doctrine explains when it speaks of eternal damnation or hell. It is not a punishment imposed externally by God but a development of premises already set by people in this life. The very dimension of unhappiness which this obscure condition brings can in a certain way be sensed in the light of some of the terrible experiences we have suffered which, as is commonly said, make life "hell."

In a theological sense however, hell is something else: it is the ultimate consequence of sin itself, which turns against the person who committed it. It is the state of those who definitively reject the Father's mercy, even at the last moment of life.

Despite what the Church has always taught, the idea of hell continues to bother us. Not necessarily that we're concerned about going to hell, but that we would prefer to believe hell is really an outdated idea that needs to be put to rest. We begin to reason it's just an empty threat, like an older sibling talking about the bogeyman under the bed, who will pop out if the younger sibling doesn't shut up and go to sleep.

Except Jesus never lied. And Jesus talked about hell. Jesus warned us about hell. For example: "If your hand or your foot causes you to stumble, cut if off and throw it away; it is better for you to enter life maimed than to have two hands or two feet and to be thrown into the eternal fire. And if your eye causes you to stumble, tear it out and throw it away; it is better for you to enter life with one eye than to have two eyes and to be thrown into the hell of fire" (Mt 18:8-9).

A couple of points can be derived from this passage: First, the idea that one must avoid hell at all costs. Here is an excellent example of why it's so dangerous to try to interpret Scripture without the help of scholarly tradition. Sadly, these verses are ones that can lead the mentally ill and fragile to harm themselves. Scripture scholars describe phrases like this as "Oriental hyperbolic mode." That means, in the East at that time, it was common to greatly exaggerate to make one's point. (We each do that still. Millions of times.)

The second point we might derive from this passage is the idea that hell is fire. Why has the image of hell as fire remained such a constant through the centuries? Anyone working in a modern-day burn unit would have an answer to that question. There may be nothing on earth that destroys and maims and tortures—but leaves alive—like fire does.

Jesus' words meant we need to have our priorities straight. Nothing can get in the way of our wanting and working toward entering the kingdom of God, because the alternative is unthinkable. Undoubtedly, that will mean our making sacrifices. Choosing "the narrow gate" is never easy: "Enter through the narrow gate; for the gate is wide and the road is easy that leads to destruction, and there are many who take it. For the gate is narrow and the road is hard that leads to life, and there are few who find it" (Mt 7:13-14).

How Could a God of Love
Send Anyone to Hell?

The idea that our loving Father can't send anyone to hell (which, as we already noted, *he* never does) is only one of the commonsense arguments against the existence of Gehenna. Another is this: If God is everywhere (and he is), then God is in hell. If God is in hell, then hell is not the absence of God. So hell can't exist.

It's true that all existence depends on God. Not just that he made it or set its development in motion. If he did not sustain it, it would not exist. A universe, a planet, a continent, a river, a tree, a human being would cease to exist if God did not continue its existence.

So, if the soul is in hell, God is continuing to keep it in existence. And, as we'll talk about in chapter 8, later that body will be reunited with that soul. But the soul, choosing to be alone, is alone in the sense that God's presence—that supreme love—is unknown to him.

In the nineteenth century, Cardinal John Henry Newman put it this way: "Heaven would be a hell to an irreligious man."

"He Descended Into Hell"

Let's tackle another thorny item. In the Apostles' Creed we say Jesus "descended into hell." Why did he do that?

The Church Fathers said he did. They took it for granted because, in the tradition of the Old Testament, when someone was dead, he was *really* dead. He left this world and went to Sheol, the underworld. Saying Jesus went to Sheol was saying more than he was in the tomb from Friday afternoon until Sunday morning. ("Three days" in the Hebrew counting of days. About forty hours for us.)

The third-century theologian Tertullian wrote: "Christ our God, who because he was man died according to the Scriptures, and was buried according to the same Scriptures, satisfied this law, also by undergoing the form of human death in the underworld, and did not ascend aloft to heaven until he had gone down to the regions beneath the earth" (*De Anima*, 55).

"Hell" in this case was not the place of the condemned, but where the faithful who had died before Jesus waited to enter heaven. Waited? Yes.

Remember that after sin entered the world, we humans were unable to be completely with God—be in heaven—until Jesus came to set things right again. The condition of these souls wasn't what we call purgatory. (That's the topic of chapter 7.) They weren't being prepared to enter heaven. Rather, heaven was unattainable for all until Jesus also entered Sheol, which he knew he was going to do.

And in fact, Scripture scholars say, the parable of the rich man and Lazarus (not to be confused with Jesus' friend with the same name) (Lk 16:19-31), as well as Old Testament references (see Is 66:22-24; Wis 3:1-12; Dn 12:2-3), indicate the intermediate state of Sheol was seen as two separate places. One for the just and one for the wicked. (The most highly favored of the just "rested in the bosom of Abraham—" that is, had a spot right next to him at the banquet table.)

Jesus knew he was headed for Sheol. "For just as Jonah was three days and three nights in the belly of the sea monster, so for three days and three nights the Son of Man will be in the heart of the earth" (Mt 12:40). He uses a quote from Jonah 2:1

which, biblical scholars note, only approximately indicates the actual amount of time between Jesus' death and resurrection.

So when, in the Apostles' Creed, we say Jesus "suffered ... was crucified, died ... was buried ... [and] descended into hell," we're acknowledging a completely human experience. Theologians emphasize that Christ gave himself totally, not just to pain and to death but to what comes after death, obediently allowing his soul to enter that shadow land, that netherworld.

Easter is Christ conquering death, Christ conquering Sheol. "I was dead, and see, I am alive forever and ever; and I have the keys of Death and of Hades" (Rv 1:18).

"Next!"

Obviously we don't know what those souls who entered heaven then experienced. It's tempting to be a bit facetious and imagine each one being given a number as he or she waited to be processed, from Adam and Eve down to someone who passed away during that first Holy Week.

Again, we're stymied by our meager minds, but maybe it's better to imagine it as a group standing in a field on a cloudy day. Suddenly the cloud burns off and all are in the sunshine. Suddenly—wondrously, miraculously—the souls of the just were in the full presence of their Creator. They, in that instant, had attained the beatific vision.

But what of the others? What about "the wicked"? What is hell *really* like? Who is *really* there? And what do we, what do you, what do I, have to do to *really* avoid the same fate?

Hell is painful. Now there's an understatement. But, to again quote Pope John Paul II, "the images of hell that Sacred

Scripture presents to us must be correctly interpreted. They show the complete frustration and emptiness of life without God. Rather than a place, hell indicates the state of those who freely and definitively separate themselves from God, the source of all life and joy."

The images we have from Scripture, even the ones Jesus used, can't compare to the reality. We can imagine unbearable heat. We've all felt tremendous physical pain, if only for a moment, when we've smacked a thumb with a hammer or banged our heads on an open cupboard door. But hell is beyond that. Hell is beyond the tooth that needs a root canal, the slipped disc, the blinding migraine, the crippling cancer or chronic depression.

Hell has no equal on earth.

All is lost in hell. No faith. No hope. No love. We have said, we have lived a life that proved, "I choose me over you, God." And God has answered, "Then you shall have you. Only you. Forever." That's what Lucifer chose just before he was cast out of heaven along with the other rebellious angels. It is loneliness to the *n*th degree. It is complete despair. It is never-ending frustration. Maybe it would help if we stopped talking so much about hell's "heat" and realized it is a cold, cold place.

Any discussion on hell would be incomplete without talking about the devil, the fallen angel Lucifer, and his demons. So, what about him? Is Satan real? Yes. And does he have power and influence in this world? Yes. And do we need to fear him? No, not in the sense that he is in any way an equal to God and God's power. But, yes, in the way we would fear anyone or anything extremely dangerous. *(Go to: "What's the Deal With ... Devils?")*

Who Has Signed the Guest Registry?

Do we know for sure of any souls that are in hell right now? Can we name some names? The Church has declared some souls in heaven. These are our canonized saints. But it never says, it can't say, who might be in hell. The Church isn't able to make that judgment. Certainly each of us, individually, can't do that.

For all we know, hell may contain no souls. How so?

We have no way of knowing who, at that moment of death, came to the realization of how he or she had offended God and others and begged forgiveness. Yes, but what about the dictator responsible for the murder of millions? What about the serial killer or the child abuser?

We cannot judge. If we ask God to be less than merciful, how can we later plead for mercy ourselves? "Let anyone among you who is without sin be the first to throw a stone at her" (Jn 8:7). You see, we're all guilty, to various degrees. And, Jesus told us to pray, "Forgive us our debts [or trespasses], as we also have forgiven our debtors [those who trespass against us]" (Mt 6:12).

Me? Forgive that person? It's not always easy to do. Sometimes, when an individual has harmed us (or someone we love) in unspeakable ways, it seems impossible to imagine finding the will to forgive that person on our own. But we are not alone. We have the Father, the Son and the Spirit. While we may never be able to forget, by God's grace we can be released from the bonds of unforgiveness.

What about suicide? We shouldn't despair that those who have taken their own lives are condemned to hell, the *Catechism* says. First it notes that while taking one's own life is contrary to a love for the God who gives life, serious psychological disturbances, anguish or grave fear of hardship, suffering or torture can diminish the responsibility of the one committing the act.

Then it explains that "by ways known to him alone, God can provide the opportunity for salutary repentance." (*Salutary* means "health giving" or "beneficial.") "The Church prays for persons who have taken their own lives" (*CCC*, 2283).

That's All, Folks

So what do we *really* have to do to avoid making hell our fate? First, it should be said that "fate" is a poor choice of words. None of us is predestined for hell (*CCC*, 1037). Yes, God knows all things and knows how we will choose, but he doesn't force us to choose. He doesn't stack the deck against us. To take that analogy one step further, it could be argued he always gives us the cards we ask for.

No, we choose hell by willfully turning away from God, that is, committing a mortal sin (we talked about those in chapter 3) and persisting in that sin until death. The *Catechism* notes that at Mass the Church always calls on God's mercy, knowing our Creator doesn't want "any to perish, but all to come to repentance" (2 Pt 3:9): "Grant us your peace in this life," says the prayer in the Roman Missal, "save us from final damnation, and count us among those you have chosen."

The Church also reminds us that we don't know when our life will end, when it will be too late.

In *Lumen Gentium*, the bishops wrote: "Since ... we know not the day nor the hour, on our Lord's advice we must be constantly vigilant so that, having finished the course of our earthly life (cf. Heb 9:27), we may merit to enter into the marriage feast with him and to be numbered among the blessed (cf. Mt 25:31-46), and that we may not be ordered to go into eternal fire (cf. Mt 25:41) like the wicked and slothful servant (cf. Mt. 25:26), into the exterior darkness where 'there will be the weeping and gnashing of teeth' (Mt 22:13; 25:30)" (48).

We have only one lifetime to accept God, if even imperfectly. And we don't know when that life will end. Then, if by our actions we have demonstrated we don't want to be with God, he honors our request.

But if we have attempted to turn back to him, sought forgiveness for our serious—our mortal, our truly deadly—sins, if we have tried to love him and serve him by serving others then ... then even though our souls, our very selves, are not ready for heaven, we are not headed for hell.

If that's the case, we need to become better at loving, which is what happens in purgatory.

What's the Deal With ... Devils?

Q: Who or what is the devil, and how did he come to be?

The devil and other demons are angels who became evil by their own doing. "God did not spare the angels when they sinned, but cast them into hell and committed them to chains of deepest darkness" (2 Pt 2:4). Their fall was a free choice to completely and eternally reject God.

Q: What do you mean "the devil and other demons"?

According to Scripture and Church teaching, Satan, or the devil, tempted our first parents to commit that first sin. But there are also other fallen angels, demons. We get the name *Satan* from the Hebrew for "accuser" (in a court of law) or "adversary." In Hebrew he is "the Satan." In Greek the word was translated *dia-bolos,* meaning "one who throws himself across God's plans," or we would say, opposes God. That's where we get *devil.*

Q: Where are these demons?

They are in hell, which (as we noted in this chapter) can better be described as a state of being rather than a particular physical location. That means they can also be on this earth.

Q: Does the devil have horns and a tail and use a pitchfork?

Being an angel, Satan is a spirit. He has no body. The horns, tail, pitchfork, cloven hooves, red jumpsuit and all the rest are artistic interpretations. They're ones that, it seems safe to speculate, please him these days. After all, if you seem to be at best a cartoon, why should people fear you or even believe in your existence?

Q: Can the devil make me do something?

Satan can't force you to commit a sin. You have free will. He can, however, tempt you. No human has been exempt from that, not even Jesus (see Mt 4:3-10).

Q: Can the devil harm me?

Satan's power is finite but "his action may cause grave injuries—of a spiritual nature and, indirectly, even of a physical nature—to each man and to society" (*CCC,* 395).

Q: What is an exorcism?

That's when the Church asks publicly and authoritatively in the name of Jesus that a person or object be protected against the power of Satan and "withdrawn from his dominion" (*CCC,* 1673).

Jesus performed exorcisms, and that's where the Church gets the power to do so. A simple form is used at every baptism when we're asked if we reject Satan. A "major exorcism" can be performed only by a priest with the permission of a bishop, strictly following the rules established by the Church.

In the ancient world, many unexplained maladies were attributed to demonic possession. In our own time, the *Catechism* is careful to point out: "Illness, especially psychological illness, is a very different matter; treating this is the concern of medical science. Therefore, before an exorcism is performed, it is important to ascertain that one is dealing with the presence of the Evil One, and not an illness" (1673) (cf. *CIC*, can. 1172).

Q: Should I be afraid of the devil?

More aware than afraid. "Discipline yourselves, keep alert. Like a roaring lion your adversary the devil prowls around, looking for someone to devour. Resist him, steadfast in your faith" (1 Pt 5:8-9).

Ten on Hell and Satan

An ever-burning Gehenna will burn up the condemned, and a punishment devouring with living flames.... Too late they will believe in eternal punishment who would not believe in eternal life.

—St. Cyprian (c. 210-58)

The perpetual death of the damned, that is, their separation from the life of God, will go on without end.

—St. Augustine (354-430)

To dread hell.

—St. Benedict (c. 480-547)

The pit of hell is as deep as despair.

Abbot William of St. Thierry (c.1085-1148)

Relinquish all hope, ye who enter here.

Dante Alighieri (1265-1321)

Heav'n has no rage, like love to hatred turn'd,
Nor Hell a fury, like a woman scorn'd.

—William Congreve (1670-1729)

Then I saw there was a way to hell, even from the gates of heaven.

—John Bunyan (1628-88)

The devil comes and tempts all the servants of God.

Shepherd of Hermas (second century)

The devil was an angel, and having become an apostate [one who rejects God] he induced as many of the angels as possible to fall away with him.

Origen (c. 185-c. 254)

The devil's snare does not catch you unless you are first caught by the devil's bait.

St. Ambrose (c. 340-97)

Chapter Seven

Purgatory: Summer School for the Soul

While raising our three children, my wife and I began many family meals with a single word: "Hands."

It was a final reminder that they had to wash before eating. Our daughter usually answered, "Already did." Our younger son most often got up and headed for the bathroom sink. And our older son typically held out his paws and said nothing, offering proof they were clean.

Which, most of the time, they weren't. A young boy's definition of "clean" and the true definition (a parent's) can be a long, long way from each other. So he would be banished to the bathroom. He wasn't in danger of losing his meal. He just couldn't have it yet. He wasn't ready.

That's purgatory. Kind of.

It is, in the sense that God is telling us we're not ready to sit down at the heavenly banquet yet. A place is reserved for us, but we have some cleaning up to do. We simply aren't presentable. It's as if they're in formal wear and we have on our gardening clothes after just fertilizing the roses.

That doesn't mean heaven is reserved for the la-di-da. We have to keep in mind God loves us no matter what. He never stops loving us. (He loves the souls in hell. He loves Satan. He *is* love.) No, it's more that out of our love for him, out of our respect for him, we want to look—to be—our best before joining him at his table.

Obviously these analogies fall short because purgatory doesn't have to do with how we look but how we *are*. It has to do with our capabilities, not our appearance.

In a general audience in the summer of 1999, Pope John Paul II put it this way: "As we have seen ... [in the previous two weekly talks], on the basis of the definitive option for or against God, the human being finds he faces one of these alternatives: either to live with the Lord in eternal beatitude, or to remain far from his presence."

Heaven or hell.

"For those who find themselves in the condition of being open to God, but still imperfectly, the journey toward full beatitude requires a purification, which the faith of the Church illustrates in the doctrine of 'Purgatory.'"

Says Who?

But where did the Church come up with this? And why don't all Christian denominations believe in it? The answer to both is the Bible. "In Sacred Scripture," the pope said, "we can grasp certain elements that help us to understand the meaning of this doctrine, even if it is not formally described. They express the belief that we cannot approach God without undergoing some kind of purification."

But because the "Protestant Bible" doesn't include the second book of Maccabees, which comes the closest to addressing explicitly the idea of a purgatory, it's a teaching Protestants reject. (*Go to: "What's the Deal With ... Two Bibles?"*) Then, too, as we'll see in just a bit, the doctrine was being badly abused and misused at the time of the Reformation.

The twelfth chapter of Second Maccabees says: "Therefore he made atonement for the dead, so that they might be delivered from their sin" (12:45). The military leader Judas Maccabeus did that by seeing to it that his army prayed for fallen comrades and made offerings on their behalf. It had been while moving the bodies that the soldiers had discovered that "under the tunic of each" corpse were "sacred tokens of the idols of Jamnia, which the law forbids the Jews to wear" (12:40). In other words, these men had died nobly but while in sin.

Even though Second Maccabees is the only Old Testament book that addresses the idea of purgatory so clearly, the elements of the doctrine can be found in a number of other passages. (In fact, John Paul II never referred to Maccabees in his talk on purgatory.) Leviticus notes how, according to Old Testament religious law, what is destined for God must be perfect. That has an impact both on animals to be sacrificed (22:22) and on the priests or ministers of worship (21:17-23).

The pope put it this way: "Total dedication to the God of the Covenant, along the lines of the great teachings found in Deuteronomy (cf. 6:5), and which must correspond to this physical integrity, is required of individuals and society as a whole (cf. 1 Kgs 8:61). It is a matter of loving God with all one's being, with purity of heart and the witness of deeds (1 Kgs 10:12 ff)."

After death, we need that "integrity"—that total love—to enter into perfect and complete union with God, the pope said. And those of us who don't yet have it "must undergo purification."

St. Paul suggests that, the pontiff pointed out. "The apostle speaks of the value of each person's work which will be revealed on the day of judgment." And he says: "If the work which any man has built on the foundation [which is Christ] survives, he will receive a reward. If any man's work is burned up, he will suffer loss, though he himself will be saved, but only as through fire" (1 Cor 3:14-15).

So, the Holy Father continued, at times, to reach a state of "perfect integrity" a person's intercession or mediation is needed. He offered this example: Moses obtains pardon for the people with a prayer in which he recalls the saving work done by God in the past, and prays for God's fidelity to the oath made to his ancestors (cf. Ex 32:30, 11-13).

And the figure of the Servant of the Lord, outlined in the Book of Isaiah, is also portrayed by his role of intercession and expiation for many. At the end of his suffering he "will see the light" and "will justify many," bearing their iniquities (cf. Is 52:13-53:12, especially 53:11).

The pope added that Psalm 51 can be considered, according to the perspective of the Old Testament, "as a synthesis of the process of reintegration." That is, the sinner confesses and recognizes his guilt (v. 3), asking insistently to be purified or "cleansed" (vv. 2, 9-10, 17) so he or she can proclaim the divine praise (v. 15).

In the New Testament

Those "elements" of the doctrine aren't limited to the Old Testament. In the New Testament, the pontiff said, Christ is presented as "the intercessor who assumes the functions of high priest on the day of expiation (cf. Heb 5:7; 7:25)."

But in Jesus the priesthood is presented in a new and definitive form. He "enters the heavenly shrine once and for all, to intercede with God on our behalf (cf. Heb 9:23-26, especially v. 24)." He is both priest and "'victim of expiation' for the sins of the whole world (cf. 1 Jn 2:2)."

Jesus, as the great intercessor who atones for us, will fully reveal himself at the end of our life when he will express himself with the offer of mercy, but also with the inevitable judgment for those who refuse the Father's love and forgiveness.

But, John Paul added, this offer of mercy doesn't exclude the duty to present ourselves to God, pure and whole, rich in that love which Paul calls a "[bond] of perfect harmony (Col 3:14)."

In following the Gospel exhortation to be perfect like the heavenly Father (cf. Mt 5:48) during our earthly life, we're called to grow in love, to be sound and flawless before God the Father "at the coming of our Lord Jesus with all his saints" (1 Thes 3:13f.).

And, on top of that, we're invited to "cleanse ourselves from every defilement of body and spirit" (2 Cor 7:1; cf. 1 Jn 3:3), because—to quote the Holy Father—"the encounter with God requires absolute purity."

Getting Ready to See God

Purgatory is yet another good example of the development of doctrine. As mentioned in chapters 1 and 5, through Christ we humans have everything we need to know to get to heaven. Even so, it has taken us time to understand what we were taught. In fact, we're still figuring that out. And each age must learn how to apply Christ's teaching to the particular circumstances of that era.

With regards to purgatory, the *Catechism* explains that from its beginning the Church has honored the memory of the dead and offered prayers "in suffrage for them, above all the Eucharistic sacrifice, so that, thus purified, they may attain the beatific vision of God" (*CCC*, 1032). [Cf. Council of Lyons II (1247): DS 856].

"Suffrage" doesn't have anything to do with suffering. Typically, it means the right to vote. In this context, it's prayers on the behalf of the dead.

The *Catechism* refers the reader to writings from the Council of Lyons in 1274. But long before that gathering of bishops, the early theologians had written about purgatory. Origen (c. 185-c. 254) put it this way:

> For if on the foundation of Christ you have built not only gold and silver and precious stones, (1 Cor 3:11-12) but also wood and hay and stubble, what do you expect when the soul shall be separated from the body? Would you enter into heaven with your wood and hay and stubble and thus defile the kingdom of God...? It remains then that you be committed to the fire which will burn the light materials.... But this fire consumes not the creature, but what the creature has himself built.... It is manifest that the fire destroys the wood of our transgressions, and then returns to us the reward of our works.

Obviously, Origen's description isn't to be taken literally. But he does clarify this idea of fire as something that cleanses. Anyone who works with precious metals knows that's how they are purified. Going through the process repeatedly continues to separate—and eliminate—the imperfections.

It's important to keep in mind this "fire" is not hell. The *Catechism* is very clear on this. The "final purification of the elect"—those who will be going to heaven—"is entirely different from the punishment of the damned" (*CCC*, 1031) [cf. Council of Florence (1439): DS 1304; Council of Trent (1563): DS 1820; (1547): 1580; see also Benedict XII, *Benedictus Deus* (1336): DS 1000].

St. Ambrose said the same thing in the fourth century: "But this fire whereby ... casual sins are burnt away ... is different from that which the Lord has assigned to the devil and his angels, of which he says, 'Enter into everlasting fire.'"

What are "casual sins"? As discussed in chapter 3, these are the ones we would call venial. The ones that aren't "deadly." St. Gregory the Great, the pope from 590 to 604, referred to them as "lesser faults." He wrote: "As for certain lesser faults, we must believe that, before the Final Judgment, there is a purifying fire. He who is truth says that whoever blasphemes against the Holy Spirit will be pardoned neither in this age nor in the age to come. From this sentence we understand that certain offenses can be forgiven in this age, but certain others in the age to come."

That, of course, raises another question: What is a sin against the Holy Spirit? What does it mean to "speak against" the Third Person of the Blessed Trinity (Mt 12:31)? The Church says it's deliberately refusing to accept God's mercy by repenting and it's rejecting the forgiveness of one's sins and the salvation offered by the Spirit (*CCC,* 1864). That hardness of heart can lead to final impenitence (not repenting) and eternal loss.

On the other hand, even "smaller" sins take a toll and merit temporal punishment. That's why "the Church also commends almsgiving, indulgences, and works of penance undertaken on behalf of the dead" (*CCC,* 1032).

Almsgiving means money for the poor. Penance is making a sacrifice such as going without a favorite treat. But indulgences ...

Heaven! On Sale! Now!

Unfortunately, there have been times when what the Church teaches has been misconstrued, misunderstood or just plain ignored. Worse still, the ideas of indulgences and purgatory have been used by the unscrupulous to browbeat people into submission or get them to empty their pockets.

It's easy to misunderstand what indulgences are all about, especially since the whole concept was badly abused in the late Middle Ages. Then they were peddled by some as Get-Out-of-Hell-Free cards. You could be a completely rotten person, but with an indulgence tucked away, you were guaranteed eternal life.

Or so the promoters claimed.

Hucksters—clerical and otherwise—also pushed them as Buy-Your-Loved-Ones-Out-of-Purgatory cards.

In 1343 Pope Clement VI sanctioned the belief that Jesus and the saints have left a treasury of merits on which other members of the Church can draw for the remission of temporal punishment due to sin. (We'll cover that in just a bit.) A person got his share of these merits by a Church indulgence, which was usually granted by the pope in exchange for a good work. Often that was making a donation of money. Doctrine always said that *the work needed to be accompanied by interior repentance.*

But that very important point tended to be overlooked or ignored.

Eventually the doctrine was applied to the souls in purgatory, too. As members of the mystical Body of Christ, they could take advantage of the merits of the saints. *(Go to: "What's the Deal With ... Indulgences?")*

What's the Deal With ... Indulgences?

Q: What's an indulgence?

An indulgence is a remission before God of the temporal punishment, for the guilt of sins has already been forgiven. Sins that have already been confessed and absolved.

Q: Are there different kinds of indulgences?

They can be partial or "plenary"—complete. They can be gained only for oneself or for the souls in purgatory, but not for another living person.

Q: Where do they come from?

Indulgences are derived from what is called "the treasury of merits" of the saints, from Jesus and from Mary. Crudely put, we all belong to the same co-op and what they have put into it is, under particular conditions, available to us.

Q: Some prayers have "100 days indulgence" or "300 days indulgence" noted after them. What does that mean?

Saying that prayer, or performing some act, is the equivalent to that amount of time performing penance in the ancient Church. In the old days, penances given during confession could be more than a few Our Fathers or Hail Marys. A lot more.

Q: So this is all ancient history, not currently being practiced?

Oh, no, indulgences are still around. In our own time it's easy to dismiss them as some quaint, outdated custom. But they're still valuable.

As recently as 1999 a revised *Enchiridion Indulgentiarum*— or manual of indulgences—was released by the Vatican.

Q: What's a "plenary indulgence"?

If you die immediately after receiving a plenary indulgence, you skip purgatory.

Q: Why?

It's a "remission before God"—a pardon, a forgiveness in God's eyes—of the temporal punishment due to sin.

Q: What's that?

To understand what the Church teaches about indulgences, it's necessary to understand that sin has a double consequence.

Grave sin deprives us of communion with God and so makes us incapable of eternal life. Being deprived of that is called the "eternal punishment" of sin. (All this and what follows can be found in no. 1472 in the *Catechism*.)

As we said before, a big-time sin (a "mortal," deadly, sin) is our saying "no thanks" to God and his offer of heaven. Since he gives us free will, he *really* lets us choose him or reject him, and he honors our decision.

Q: What about small sins?

Every sin, even venial, includes an "unhealthy attachment to creatures." That is, to created stuff—loving things more than God and our fellow human beings. That fault must be corrected and purified, either here on earth, or after death, in the state called purgatory.

Q: Why?

Again, every sin in some way or another is our putting money, power, pleasure, toys—whatever—ahead of love of God and neighbor. Which isn't to say money, power, pleasure, toys and whatever are in themselves bad. It's that they can be, depending on how we use them or let them use us.

The *Catechism* explains that this purification frees one from what is called the "temporal punishment" of sin. These two punishments, here on earth and in purgatory, must not be thought of as a kind of vengeance inflicted by God from without, but as following from the very nature of sin.

A conversion which naturally flows from a "fervent charity" can attain the complete purification of the sinner in such a way that no punishment would remain.

In the Middle Ages

The problem with how indulgences were being presented to the public during the Middle Ages was that the ideas of personal repentance and personal responsibility were brushed aside. It was the promoting of indulgences in this way that helped launch Martin Luther and the Reformation.

Historians say that at that time an indulgence was being preached and sold supposedly to help raise money to rebuild St. Peter's Basilica. In reality, the money went to a banking firm, the Roman Curia, and the twenty-three-year-old archbishop of Mainz, Germany. Luther, a member of the Augustinian order, was a professor and village parish priest in a neighboring diocese.

Father Luther didn't condemn the idea of indulgences, just how they were being misused. Even so, the situation escalated from there. He was ready and willing to debate his theses, but his opponents refused. The Mainz archbishop reported him to Rome. The fellow Dominicans of the principal preacher of the indulgence, Johann Tetzel, declared it was a matter of authority and told Luther to simply accept it.

On the other hand, the majority of Luther's fellow Augustinians came to agree with Luther's point of view. And the pontiff at the time, Leo X, was busy with things happening in Italy and assumed the whole affair was not much more than a tiff between monks.

No doubt some things that were happening at that time in the name of the Church needed to be reformed. And it wasn't just those who became Protestant who were calling for it. So were some who remained in the Church and even later were declared saints (Teresa of Avila, for example).

Unfortunately, the issue of indulgences and, with it, the concept of purgatory, became one of *the* issues. One group rejected it. Another, even while perhaps not fully understanding it, defended it vigorously.

In a nutshell, that's the legacy we have inherited, Protestant and Catholic alike. It seems safe to say the average Protestant or Catholic would profess what his denomination teaches with regard to purgatory, even while being unsure what that teaching is or why it's taught.

So let's be more specific.

Brass Tacks Purgatory

What is purgatory? Like heaven and hell, we need to think of purgatory as a state of being. In that condition, we are sorry for our sins. We are, it seems safe to speculate, embarrassed by them. In it, perhaps, we see clearly the ramifications of our selfishness— not just how we have offended God but how we have injured others. The far-reaching, rippling effects of all our selfishness.

Is purgatory painful? Yes, if admitting mistakes and realizing how we've hurt others causes us pain. And since it does on earth, why wouldn't it where we are becoming better at loving? Where we are getting rid of our attachment to what isn't good? Again, on earth, any personal growth or change is typically accompanied by fear and anxiety. In that sense, being in purgatory can be compared to being a precious metal that is purified in a fire (but that doesn't mean it has fire as we know it).

How long does a soul stay in purgatory? We don't know, although with God, a day can be as a thousand years and a thousand years a day (2 Pt 3:8). Time really is relative. It passes quickly when we're having fun and seems to stand still when we're in pain, whether physical or emotional.

Who is in purgatory? We can't say.

Are the souls in purgatory miserable? Yes, because of that pain. And no, because they know—they are guaranteed—one day they will enter heaven and spend eternity with God. St. Catherine of Genoa (1447-1510) put it this way:

Souls in purgatory unite great joy with great suffering. One does not diminish the other. No peace is comparable to that of the souls in purgatory, except that of the saints in heaven. On the other hand, the souls in purgatory endure torments which no tongue can describe and no intelligence comprehend, without special revelation.

Along those same lines, Pope John Paul stressed:

Those who live in this state of purification after death are not separated from God but are immersed in the love of Christ. Neither are they separated from the saints in heaven—who already enjoy the fullness of eternal life—nor from us on earth—who continue on our pilgrim journey to the Father's house. We all remain united in the Mystical Body of Christ, and we can therefore offer up prayers and good works on behalf of our brothers and sisters in purgatory.

In fact, the Church has set aside a feast for them. Each year it celebrates All Souls' Day on November 2, only one day after the feast of All Saints.

What's the Deal With ... Two Bibles?

Q: Why are there two different Bibles?

The "Catholic" and "Protestant" Old Testaments aren't identical.

Q: What's the difference?

Protestants don't have the books of Tobit, Judith, Wisdom, Sirach, Baruch, 1 and 2 Maccabees, the last six chapters of Esther and three passages from Daniel.

Q: Why not?

All of those are in what's called the Alexandrian version of sacred writing translated into Greek between 250 and 100 B.C. and in use by Greek-speaking Jews outside Palestine.

But the Hebrew canon (*canon* means "list"), fixed by tradition and the consensus of rabbis by about 100 B.C., was used by the Palestinian community. Catholics have used the first one. Protestants, since Luther, who translated the entire Bible into German, chose the second.

Q: What about the New Testament?

They're the same for both.

Ten on Purgatory

When he has quitted his body and the difference between virtue and vice is known he cannot approach God till the purging fire shall have cleansed the stains with which his soul is infested.

—St. Gregory of Nyssa (c. 335-95)

To some, what is not remitted in this world is remitted in the world to come.

—St. Augustine (354-430)

God holds them in the furnace until every defect has been burnt away and he has brought them each in his own degree to a certain standard of perfection.

—St. Catherine of Genoa (1447-1510)

There is a purgatory and ... souls there detained are helped by the intercession of the faithful.

—Council of Trent (1563)

I hold unswervingly that there is a purgatory.

—Tridentine Profession of Faith (1564)

If purgatory is a species of hell as regards suffering, it is even more a species of paradise as regards heavenly love and sweetness.

—Bishop Jean Pierre Camus (1582-1652)

Help, Lord, the souls which thou has made,
    The souls to thee so dear,
In prison, for the debt unpaid
    Of sins committed here.

—Cardinal John Henry Newman (1801-90)

O turn to Jesus, Mother! turn,
   And call him by his tenderest names;
Pray for the holy souls that burn
   This hour amid the cleansing flames.

—Frederick Faber (1814-63)

The existence of purgatory naturally implies the correlative dogma—the utility of praying for the dead.

—Cardinal James Gibbons (1834-1921)

We believe that the souls of all those who die in the grace of Christ, whether they must still be purified in purgatory or whether from the moment they leave their bodies Jesus takes them to Paradise as he did for the good thief, are the people of God in the eternity beyond death.

—Pope Paul VI (1897-1978)

Chapter Eight

Final Judgment:
The Lightning Round

I confess that if the mystery I'm reading isn't grabbing my attention I'll jump to the end of the book to find out who the murderer is.

Sometimes we all like to skip to the end, to fast-forward. But when it comes to the end of the world, the end of time, we don't have to do that. Jesus has already given away the ending.

That's why the classic magazine cartoon prophet on the busy city sidewalk—the tall, skinny fellow with the long beard and robe—is absolutely correct when his sign reads, "The world is coming to an end."

The world *is* coming to an end. Someday (in the words of cultural icon Gomer Pyle, "Surprise, surprise, surprise!"), there won't be a tomorrow.

What does that mean for us, both those who are still on the earth and those who have died? In a sense, like one of Shakespeare's plays, it will be the opening of Act V.

Cue the lightning.

If all the world is a stage, and we are but players on it (and almost all of us bit players and walk-ons in the big picture of history), then a cosmic program might read:

Curtain up.

Act I: Creation

Act II: Sin

Act III: Jesus

Act IV: The Church

Act V: Jesus Returns

Curtain down.

As with any good story, the last act is going to be a dilly. And the postproduction party is going to last forever. We know some things about both—quite a bit really. But specifics escape us. We've been given some of the what by Jesus and his Church. And we have a lot of the why. But our information is very thin when it comes to the when and the how.

The when *really* interests us. It fascinates us. In every age there is a leader who attracts others by proclaiming the when. Whether it's a doomsday cult that self-destructs in mass suicide or sincere Christians who have their spiritual bags packed because our calendar says we're starting a new millennium, the leader is only guessing, at best. Or deceiving for personal gain, at worst.

Jesus couldn't have been more direct: Only God knows.

The Church's teaching on the end of the world falls under a general category called "last things." Its proper name is "eschatology," from the Greek *eschata* for "end" or "outcome." Its pillars are death, judgment, heaven and hell. But it also covers purgatory and limbo.

You may notice that we've already covered most of those, too. So now we'll look more closely at the end of the world. And we'll revisit judgment, since it has two parts: personal and general.

-The End-

But first, the end of the world. Literally. How will we know it's happening? Keep in mind, it could happen in our own time.

The world could end later today. Or tomorrow. Or the day after.

On the other hand, it could happen thousands of years from now. Or hundreds of thousands of years. Or millions. (We speak of the first centuries after Christ as "the early Church." But, as some folks have pointed out, many, many years from now Christians may include our own time under that general heading.)

In any case, it's good that we keep *our* spiritual bags packed. That doesn't mean that we should just sit by the door and wait for Jesus to come again. Or that we are to be indifferent to the needs of others, since none of this matters anyway. After all, that reasoning goes, everything will be swept away, so why get excited about anything in this world?

Packing Those Spiritual Bags

One of the most basic and necessary ways that we can pack our spiritual bags, center our lives on Christ, is serving others. Please note: This is *very* important. Few things in your life—you who are reading these words—are as important.

Why?

There will come a time, at the end of time, when you will be in front of Jesus and every other soul ever created. And he will ask you to unpack.

Obviously, that's only an analogy. But it's also a reality.

Another done deal.

It's easy to dismiss this end-of-the-world business as nothing more than primitive mumbo jumbo. Like pious legends about medieval saints, more fanciful than fact.

It ain't that way.

At the end of time:

—Every body will rise from the dead and be reunited with his or her soul.

—Jesus will return to earth.

—You will face general judgment.

—The universe will be renewed. (*Go to: "What's the Deal With ... Cosmos II: The Sequel?"*)

My Body Is Going to *What?*

This business (about the body and soul being reunited) is hard to understand. Hard to believe. It doesn't make sense to us in the twenty-first century. It didn't make sense to some of Jesus' contemporaries in the first century, either. At that time, the Pharisees believed in the resurrection of the body. But another influential group, the Sadducees, didn't.

Again, we have the advantage of hindsight. It's easier for us to believe because, as the *Catechism* notes: "We shall rise like Christ, with him and through him" (995).

Even so, down through the ages some folks have considered this doctrine one of the Church's most foolish. There have been those who carried their contempt beyond death. They were cremated as a final "says you, pal!" reasoning that even God himself can't reassemble ashes. (That was why, for a time, cremation was against Church law. That's changed recently with the note that cremation is *not* allowed if its purpose is to thumb one's nose at belief in the resurrection of the body.)

Who could argue that bodies returning from the dead isn't an amazing teaching? A jaw-dropping assertion.

Again, as if we needed more evidence of how much God loves us, here it is: Not only can our souls live for eternity in complete happiness, but our bodies can, too. We humans, made up of spirit and flesh, get to have both enter heaven.

But not right away. Obviously. Like John Brown's body, everyone who has died "lies a moldering in the grave," in one fashion or another. Obviously, those who died eons ago are no more than dust. And they could be less than dust.

But at the end of time, when Jesus comes again, each and every body will be reunited with his or her soul and spend eternity in heaven or hell.

Christ was the first to be raised with his own body. But he didn't return to an "earthly" body. His resurrected body differed from those he had raised from the dead during his public ministry (such as Lazarus, the brother of Martha and Mary; you can read about him in John 11:1-44). Those he raised all died again.

No, this resurrection leads to unending life for the body. When it happens, Christ "'will change our lowly body to be like his glorious body,' into a 'spiritual body'" (*CCC*, 999). [Lateran Council IV (1215); DS 801; Phil 3:21; 1 Cor 15:44.]

St. Paul Says We're Ready

This resurrection is what is scheduled to begin Act V on "the last day." And we all have a role. Center stage. None of us will be bit players, living or dead.

That's a point St. Paul makes in his second letter to the Thessalonians. In chapter 4, he first reminds the people that while they may grieve at the death of their loved ones, that isn't the end of the story. "For since we believe that Jesus died and rose again, even so, through Jesus, God will bring with him those who have died" (v. 14). St. Paul continues that, on the last day:

> We who are [still] alive, who are left until the coming of the Lord, will by no means precede those who have died. For the Lord himself, with a cry of command, with the archangel's call and with the sound of God's trumpet, will descend from heaven and the dead in Christ will rise first. Then we who are alive, who are left, will be caught up in the clouds together with them to meet the Lord in the air; and so we will be with the Lord forever.
>
> 1 THESSALONIANS 4:15-17

St. Paul offers a reminder, a warning, too. That final day will come like a thief in the night. Like a war suddenly breaking out in peacetime. Like a woman going into labor. But Christians are prepared for this, he adds. The "children of the light" aren't going to be surprised. "Awake" and "sober," they are to "put on the breastplate of faith and love, and for a helmet the hope of salvation" (5:8).

Yes, but ... this raises all kinds of questions to which we simply don't have the answers. "The 'how' exceeds our imagination and understanding," the *Catechism* says. "It is accessible only to faith. Yet our participation in the Eucharist already gives us a foretaste of Christ's transfiguration of our bodies" (*CCC*, 1000).

We'd like to know the details but, in the long run, they really don't matter. In the long run—which is eternity—to quote the fourteenth-century mystic Julian of Norwich: "All will be well."

Everything's going to be OK.

God's got a plan. God's got it covered.

Where's Jesus?

And speaking of God, or more specifically Jesus, what's this "coming again" business? Isn't he already here? God is everywhere. And Jesus is present in a particular way in the Eucharist. So what do we mean he's coming again?

Yes, God is everywhere. Yes, the resurrected body of Jesus is present in the Eucharist, but there his body is under the appearances of bread and wine. In apostolic times, how he was present after his Resurrection but before his Ascension—for instance, when he told Thomas to examine his hands and side (Jn 20:24-29)—was different from how he is present in the breaking of the bread.

All this has to do with the kingdom of God among us. With the reign of God being at hand. What will be, already is. Or more correctly, has already begun in the Church, through the sacraments.

Even as Christ redeemed us, even as he established God's kingdom and the Church, he knew he would return a second time. In his own words, recorded in Mark: "After that suffering, the sun will be darkened, and the moon will not give its light, and the stars will be falling from heaven, and the powers of the heavens will be shaken. Then they will see 'the Son of Man coming in clouds' with great power and glory. Then he will send out the angels, and gather his elect from the four winds, from the ends of the earth to the ends of heaven" (13:24-27).

Even Christ didn't know *when* this will happen. "But about that day or hour no one knows, neither the angels in heaven, nor the Son, but only the Father" (13:32).

And, as St. Paul would do later, Jesus urged his listeners to "beware" and "keep alert."

Not surprisingly, the Church has a name for the Second Coming. It's referred to as the *Parousia*, which is Greek for "presence" or "arrival." Its secular use meant the arrival of a king or emperor to a city for a royal visit. In the Old Testament it was the coming of the Messiah. In the New, it's Jesus' arrival at the end of time.

It's going to be quite a day. Resurrected bodies reunited with souls. Jesus coming again with not a little fanfare. Those still living gathered up by angels.

A truly marvelous, blessed occasion until ... ready for the bad news?

This has another name with which you may be familiar: Judgment Day.

Uh-oh.

Facing Final Judgment

Exactly. When you die you face what is known as "particular judgment." In a sense, you stand before God and, by how you led your life, you choose him—or not. Or as we talked about in chapter 7, you choose him but you just aren't spiritually mature enough to be with him and so you go to purgatory to do some growing up.

Whether you're still on earth or in heaven, hell or purgatory, "general judgment" still awaits you. That's what happens after the Second Coming.

This isn't a second shot at salvation. No soul is going to be bounced from heaven or excused from hell. No, after facing particular judgment you will know how you are going to spend eternity and will begin spending it.

Simply put, general or final judgment doesn't re-open the case. It just goes over *all* the evidence. In front of everyone. *Everyone.*

God doesn't do this because he's cruel. He isn't. He does it because he is Truth and heaven is being face to face with Truth. So there's no kidding ourselves. No sweeping items under the carpet.

On Judgment Day, you will see *exactly* how what you did, and what you failed to do, affected others. All the ramifications, which could, it seems safe to speculate, stretch out over generations and touch people you never even met.

Think about it. Let's start with a positive example: You are a loving parent who brought up your children in a nurturing home centered on Christ. They grew up with confidence and grace and became parents who brought up their children in a nurturing home....

That would be part of the big picture. But the little one matters, too. One morning on the bus you stood and offered your seat to an elderly woman. A simple, tiny act of kindness. Another commuter noticed your gesture and was impressed. Later that day, remembering the event, he made the effort to be a little more charitable to the office outcast.

And so on, and so on, and so on.

But surely God doesn't keep track of our lives *that* closely?

Surely there isn't really an angel jotting down everything with a large quill pen?

An angel ... probably not. God keeping track ... yes.

That's so despite what Shakespeare had Marc Antony say in "Julius Caesar" (Act III, Scene ii; the speech that starts "Friends, Romans, countrymen, lend me your ears"): "The evil that men do lives after them; the good is oft interred with their bones."

Maybe a much more modern analogy will help: DNA. Not how it's used as evidence at crime scenes or to determine paternity, but how it can be examined to discover ancestry that stretches back centuries.

We are imprinted, and leave an imprint, biologically.

In a sense, the same is true spiritually.

Baa, Baa

None of this is a secret. Jesus told us it's going to happen. It would have been difficult to put it in plainer or simpler language. You've probably heard it. Nodded your head in agreement to it. Thought "hmmm" and really meant to apply it.

But this isn't like some homeowner's insurance policy. You buy it but figure you'll never really have to use it. This isn't some spare tire kept in the trunk, just in case.

This is *going* to happen.

Judgment Day will come.

If you want to see what's on the agenda, check out Matthew 25:31-46. When Jesus "comes in his glory and all the angels with him," everyone—"all the nations"—are going to be gathered and separated, like sheep from goats.

In first-century Palestine, a sheep was worth more than a

young goat. In Jesus' description, the sheep go on the right; goats on the left.

Then Christ will say to the sheep, "Come on into heaven. That's your inheritance prepared for you since the beginning of the world. It's yours because when I was hungry you fed me. When I was thirsty you gave me something to drink. When I was a stranger you welcomed me. When I was naked you clothed me. When I was sick you took care of me. When I was in prison you visited me."

The sheep, "the righteous," will reply: "Huh? You ... We did...? When was that?"

Jesus will tell them: "When you did it to the least among you, you did it to me." And then he'll turn to the goats and let them know that they *didn't* do those things when he needed them done.

The goats will reply: "Huh? You ... We didn't...? When was that?"

Of course, the answer is "when you *didn't* do it to the least among you."

So the sheep enter eternal life and goats eternal punishment.

Two things to keep in mind:

First, this comes as no surprise to those who have already died. Since they have faced particular judgment, they already know the outcome. We aren't kept waiting and worrying, from the time of the death until the end of time.

Second, Jesus doesn't say, "You did this or you didn't do this to my good friends or my family or my loved ones." He says, "You did or didn't do this to *me.*"

This is the most important point in this book. It's good to examine what the Church teaches about heaven, hell and purgatory. It's better to keep those basic teachings in mind. It's best to realize that because the Messiah has come, you hold the keys that unlock those pearly gates.

Keys to the Kingdom

The most important key to the kingdom of God is this: Loving God with your whole heart, mind and soul. Loving him by loving and serving others. You could say those gates don't use keys but a combination. One that can be very easy to memorize but very difficult to live.

To put it another way, on this pilgrimage, the map is simple. But the journey is hard.

Our Creator knows this. We humans messed things up so much we were hopelessly lost. So he sent his Son. And after the Son showed us the way—after we began to realize he is the Way—then he returned to the Father and the two of them flooded their earth, flooded their Church, with the Love that is between them, the Spirit.

That's why we, so often more goat than sheep, have reason to hope.

God wants nothing more than to have you spend eternity with him.

What's the Deal With ... Cosmos II: The Sequel?

Q: What happens after general judgment?

The Church teaches, to quote *Lumen Gentium*, "at that time the human race, as well as the entire world, which is intimately related to man and attains to its end [reaches its destiny] through him, will be perfectly reestablished in Christ" (48).

Or, as Scripture puts it, "we wait for new heavens and a new earth, where righteousness is at home" (2 Pt 3:13).

Q: What does that mean for me?

For us humans, it's going to be "the final realization of the unity of the human race, which God willed from creation" (*CCC*, 1045).

"The beatific vision, in which God opens himself in an inexhaustible way to the elect [those in heaven], will be the ever-flowing well-spring of happiness, peace, and mutual communion" (*CCC*, 1045).

Q: And for the universe?

It's destined to be transformed. "Creation itself will be set free from its bondage to decay" (Rom 8:21).

That's going to happen, to quote St. Irenaeus (130-202), "so that the world itself, restored to its original state, facing no further obstacles, should be at the service of the just."

When Cosmos II begins, everything—earth, sky and us—is going to be as it should be.

As it was always meant to be.

Ten on Last Judgment

The prophets have foretold two comings of Christ: the one which has already taken place ... the other ... when he shall gloriously come from heaven with his angelic army.

—St. Justin Martyr (100-165)

There are still to come other spectacles—the last, that eternal Day of Judgment, that day the Gentiles never believed would come, that day they laughed at.

—Tertullian (c. 160-c. 222)

Do you believe in Christ Jesus, the Son of God ... who will come to judge the living and the dead? [Question put to those to be baptized.]

—St. Hippolytus (d.c. 236)

Oh, what and how great will that day be at its coming, beloved brethren.

—St. Cyprian (d. 258)

Believe ... that he is to return, glorious and illustrious.

—St. Gregory Nazianzus (c. 330-c. 390)

For when the judgment is finished, this heaven and earth shall cease to be, and there will be a new heaven and a new earth. For this world shall pass away by transmutation, not by absolute destruction.

—St. Augustine (354-430)

To fear the day of judgment.

—St. Benedict (c. 480-c. 547)

How fearful shall thy judgment be, O Lord, when angels stand around and men be there, when the books be opened and our actions shown and our intentions tried.... Who shall make my darkness light, if thou, O Lord, the Lover of mankind, do not have mercy on me?

—Byzantine prayer (c. ninth century)

The Last Judgment will reveal that God's justice triumphs over all the injustices committed by his creatures and that God's love is stronger than death (cf. *Song* 8:6).

Catechism of the Catholic Church (1997)

Christ has died. Christ is risen. Christ will come again.

—Proclamation of Faith (twentieth century)

Conclusion

After examining hell and eternal damnation, it would be easy to let fear grip us and control our lives. None of us is worthy of heaven. None of us "earns" it as a just payment for how we have lived our lives.

But we don't have to be afraid. Why? Because that just Judge separating sheep and goats, the one who has every right to give us what we truly deserve, is all-merciful.

He's the shepherd who leaves the ninety-nine to find and save each of us when we stray.

He's the shepherd by our side as we walk through the valley of the shadow of death.

He's the shepherd who lays down his life for his sheep.

He's *our* shepherd.

He's *your* shepherd.

He did it all, from the beginning of time, for you.

And you, if you listen, can hear his voice.

Pray for me as I for thee, that we may merrily meet in heaven.
—Paraphrase of quote by St. Thomas More (1478-1535)
Feast of St. Dominic
August 8, 2000